THE ZOOM FLY BOLT BLAST

STEAM HANDBOOK

Build **18** Innovative Projects with Brain Power

LANCE AKIYAMA ➕ galileo

ROCKPORT

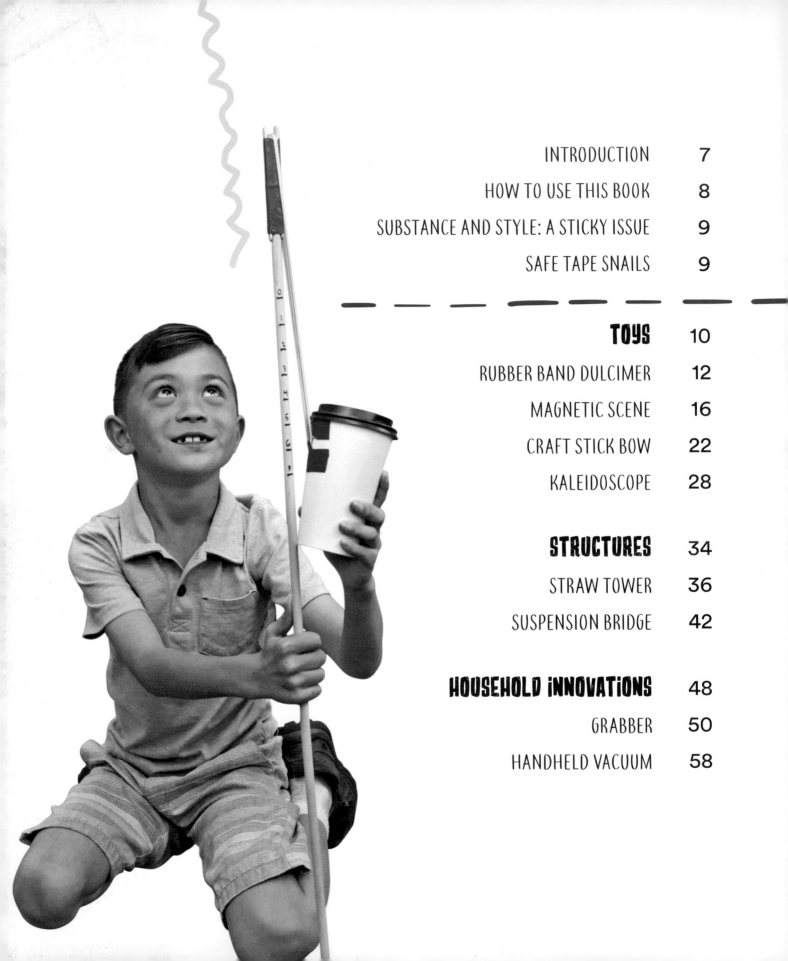

FOREWORD

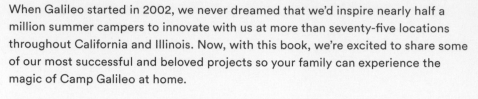

When Galileo started in 2002, we never dreamed that we'd inspire nearly half a million summer campers to innovate with us at more than seventy-five locations throughout California and Illinois. Now, with this book, we're excited to share some of our most successful and beloved projects so your family can experience the magic of Camp Galileo at home.

While the art and engineering projects in this book *do* zoom, fly, bolt, and blast, there's more to them than that. Each Galileo project is carefully designed to develop children as innovators while they create. In fact, Galileo's mission is to develop innovators who envision and create a better world.

We pursue our mission because we believe that the ability to innovate—to imagine something that does not yet exist and to have the creative confidence (and skill set) to make that vision reality—is one of the most powerful tools we can give children to prepare them for the future. This ability is shared by individuals like Thomas Edison, Dolores Huerta, Shirley Ann Jackson, and Marvin Gaye—all famous inventors, activists, or artists who envisioned and created things that transformed the world on a societal level and helped to improve countless lives.

But innovation isn't just about creating the next big tech breakthrough or social movement. At its core, being an innovator is about being an actor in the world instead of a passive recipient. It's about reflecting on a situation, recognizing the possibility for something better, and making it happen. And so, we believe innovation also exists on a deeply personal level.

If a person notices she can have a better relationship with a friend and finds a way to make that idea a reality, that's an innovation. If someone recognizes he is not in an ideal work environment and implements his ideas to make things better, that person is thinking and acting like an innovator. If someone seizes an opportunity to improve something they do every day—how they get to work or school, or what they do with their free time—that's innovation, too.

Innovators are creators of desirable outcomes and have agency in their lives. They have a clear vision for what will make them happy and go and create that reality for themselves. Isn't this what we want for our children? For all children?

The good news is that the ability to innovate is not a talent that you are born with. Each of us can become more innovative by learning the well-defined skills and practices that predictably deliver innovation. At camp and in this book, we nurture innovators by infusing projects and experiences with our secret sauce: the Galileo Innovation Approach® (GIA for short).

Inspired by the design thinking framework developed at the Hasso Plattner Institute of Design at Stanford University, the GIA teaches children how to create and think like innovators. Built into every Galileo project are the three components of the GIA: 1) substantive KNOWLEDGE that guides breakthrough thinking, 2) a transformative MINDSET that promotes innovative work, and 3) a time-tested, iterative design PROCESS that supports bringing the best ideas to fruition.

We hope your family zooms, flies, bolts, and blasts its way through the projects in this book. The more projects you do, the more opportunities you'll have to practice the GIA and the more you'll come to believe in your own ability to embrace challenges, learn from mistakes, and create without fear as you make your wildest ideas come to life.

KNOWLEDGE
Innovators have the subject knowledge, historical context, skills and techniques, and empathy needed to create in their area.

GALILEO INNOVATION APPROACH®

MINDSET
Innovators embody a set of qualities that include vision, courage, determination, collaboration, and reflection.

PROCESS
Innovators know how to identify a goal, generate ideas, design, create, test, redesign, and share.

Pamela Briskman
Vice President of Education

Glen Tripp
Founder & Chief Executive Officer

Galileo Learning
Oakland, California

INTRODUCTION

Zoom, fly, bolt, blast—that's just the start of it. These contraptions jump, drive, lift, grab, float, spin, vacuum the carpet, and even play music!

Nothing is more exciting than discovering you can build something that actually gets up and moves, solves a problem, answers a question, or brings on a chain reaction. It's contagious—the more you make, the more you explore new ways of thinking, and the more innovative you become.

Science, technology, engineering, art, and math (STEAM)-based learning is recognized as the best way to prepare kids for careers in the future. It's also the best way to inspire curious minds and have ingeniously satisfying fun while doing so. The eighteen projects in this book are based on the successful curriculum of Camp Galileo, Galileo Learning's national flagship summer program for rising students Pre-K through 5th grade. From automatons to pneumatic machines, slingshot cars to suspension bridges, these projects guide kids to use their heads and their hands to generate ideas, design, create, test, evaluate, and redesign to their heart's content.

HOW TO USE THIS BOOK

The Zoom, Fly, Bolt, Blast STEAM Handbook is carefully crafted to teach innovation skills for twenty-first century kids. You *can* use these ideas simply as instructions for making fun toys, but you'll miss out on the full benefit of this book. To best support young, innovative minds, look out for these components:

Design Challenge

The Design Challenge describes the goals of the project, which can almost always be met in a wide variety of ways. Before starting the project, review the challenge with kids and keep it as a focus as you build. While all of the projects include step-by-step instructions that will support you to achieve a baseline level of success, this book intentionally avoids showing the "best" ways to solve the Design Challenge. This is because there are many possible solutions. Big learning comes from reflecting on what is and isn't working as desired and then tinkering or redesigning to make things work better.

Innovator's Mindset

The innovator's mindset has five elements (be visionary, be courageous, be collaborative, be determined, and be reflective) that support breakthrough thinking and creative work. To nurture this mindset in your child, read the mindset callouts aloud and try the accompanying strategies. For example, when the project calls for being visionary, ask kids the inspiration questions provided or be their champion when the going gets tough and they need to be determined. Showing kids the benefit of approaching their challenges with an innovator's mindset will have positive effects that last well beyond the projects they'll make with this book.

Innovator's Process

The innovator's process is an iterative sequence of steps that supports bringing ideas to reality. Every project in this book guides kids through this design process, and you'll notice that just one or two parts of the process are emphasized in each chapter. These are the steps that are most meaningful in that particular project. Make sure to draw children's attention to the process by calling out the highlighted steps by name and practicing the strategies provided. When kids learn the process vocabulary and understand how it is used to solve creative problems, they'll have a useful structure for doing things that are creative and new along with steps to help them get unstuck when they are not quite sure what to do next.

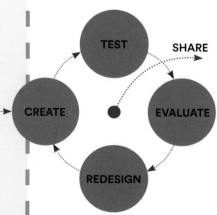

Innovator's Knowledge

The book highlights the knowledge needed to have success with each project. As you go through the book, read the concepts and facts aloud and carefully practice the pictured skills and techniques. Exploring this knowledge will help kids understand the science behind how the projects work while supporting their ability to effectively create.

SUBSTANCE AND STYLE: A STICKY ISSUE

Colorful masking tape is used in all the projects in this book because it helps make the projects look more polished. However, the tape you use is more than just an aesthetic choice. Having projects that look good and feel good to work on gives kids pride in their work and, in my opinion, helps to increase their engagement. It also adds another element of personalization.

If you also decide to go colorful with your choices, be sure to purchase good quality tape with strong adhesion. Some colorful craft tapes are sticky enough for decoration but are not made for creating these STEAM projects!

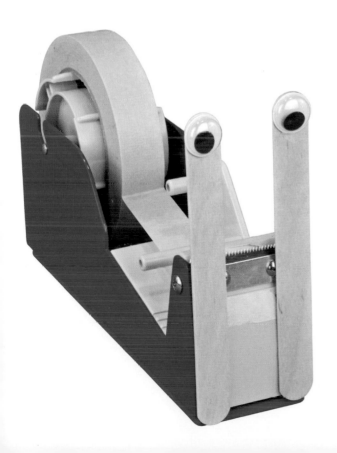

SAFE TAPE SNAILS

If you plan to conduct these projects with more than a few kids, you may find that distributing tape, particularly among those younger than 7 years of age, will be a bit of a chore. Ripping tape can be challenging for young hands, and cutting it piece-by-piece with scissors takes a long time. You could distribute tape yourself, but then you'll just be a human tape dispenser!

Instead, when working with groups of kids, I highly recommend purchasing masking tape dispensers so you and your young makers can spend more time building and less time getting tape. When ripping tape from a dispenser, the key is to pull down first, and then to the side.

Also, make sure to transform your dispenser into a Safe Tape Snail by hot gluing two craft sticks onto the front, and adding some googly eyes! This will prevent young hands from accidentally brushing against the blade—and it looks hilarious.

1

TOYS

RUBBER BAND DULCIMER

The hammered dulcimer is a string instrument with ancient roots. Unlike a guitar, however, the strings are played by hitting them with a small hammer which, in my opinion, is far more fun! Now you can build your own four-string hammered dulcimer and easily redesign your tune by moving the cups to different positions.

DESIGN CHALLENGE

Build a dulcimer that has four different and nice-sounding tones

TOOLS AND MATERIALS

» *Two pieces of 7" × 10" (18 × 25 cm) corrugated cardboard*
» *Scissors*
» *Masking tape*
» *Toilet paper tube*
» *12 oz (350 ml) paper cups*
» *⅛" × 7" (3 mm × 18 cm) rubber bands (size 117B)*
» *Durable plastic straws*

Material substitutions

If you don't have long rubber bands, you can make a smaller dulcimer with smaller rubber bands, cups, and cardboard.

PREP

Cut the cardboard.
An adult may need to help cut two pieces of cardboard into 7" × 10" (18 × 25 cm) rectangles. For extra strength, make sure the corrugations are running lengthwise, as shown in step 1.

1. Stack the two pieces of cardboard and tape them together in at least four places. This will help prevent the cardboard from bending under the tension of the rubber bands.

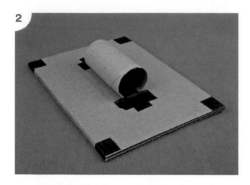

2. Attach a toilet paper tube for a handle. Use a plus-sign-shaped taping technique for extra strength: Place a piece of tape that connects the tube to the cardboard, then place another piece of tape across the first one!

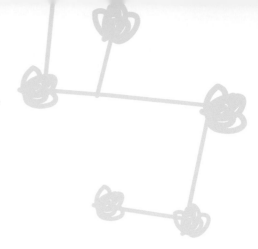

3. Rubber bands need space to vibrate. Wrap two rubber bands around the long side of the cardboard. Lift one rubber band at a time and put a cup underneath.

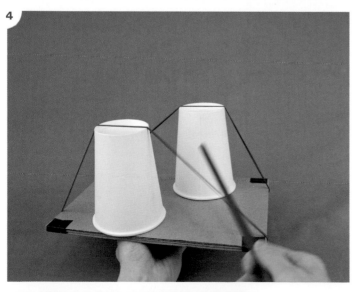

4. Play your dulcimer by swiftly tapping the rubber bands with a straw. Tap each of the four rubber bands and listen to the different tones it makes.

MINDSET: BE REFLECTIVE

5. Reflect by taking the time to notice which tones sound too similar or don't sound very nice, and change the cup position accordingly. Ask yourself: What kind of tones do long rubber band spans make? Low notes or high notes? What kind of tones do short rubber band spans make? What happens if two rubber band spans have similar lengths?

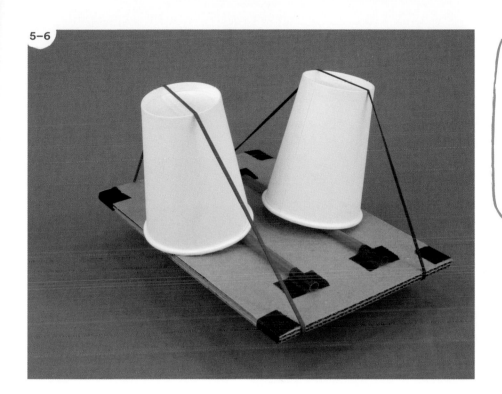

PROCESS: REDESIGN

6. Remember that your design challenge is to create four different tones that sound good. To change the tones, you need to change the length of the stretched-out rubber band spans: Just move the cups to different spots, and then play again.

7. Now redesign again!
Try taping two straws onto the cardboard so the cups are tilted to the side, then play again. What do you notice?

KNOWLEDGE: CONCEPTS AND FACTS

When the cup is tipped to the side, you might find that your dulcimer is much louder. Why? To figure that out, first, we need to know how sound works. Sound is just the air around us vibrating in different ways. Think of dropping a pebble into a puddle: You see the ripples spread across the surface. Sound is similar. For example, when you talk, you are making the air around you ripple with little sound waves. If the same kind of sound waves bump into each other, they become louder. This is called resonance. The cup acts as a resonator: When you hit the strings, the sound waves build up inside the cup. By tilting the cup on its side, you let that resonant, built-up sound escape, which makes your dulcimer louder!

MAGNETIC SCENE

A picture might be worth a thousand words, but a moving magnetic scene tells a whole story! This project uses the power of magnetic fields to push a character around a scene, as if it has a life of its own. Put on your visionary goggles and clearly imagine your scene and the story you want to tell with it!

DESIGN CHALLENGE

Build a magnetic scene that
- Tells a story
- Includes a main character
- Includes magnetic pieces of scenery that interact with the main character

TOOLS AND MATERIALS

- » *Sharpened pencil*
- » *Colorful paper*
- » *Glue stick*
- » *6" × 6" (15 × 15 cm) piece of corrugated cardboard*
- » *Scissors*
- » *Masking tape*
- » *4 drinking straws*
- » *Colorful markers*
- » *Corrugated cardboard scrap*
- » *8" (20 cm) length of cotton string*
- » *4 small (less than ½" [13 mm]) magnets*

Material substitutions

This example uses ferrite magnets because they're inexpensive. You can also use neodymium magnets (also called rare-earth magnets). These are much more powerful, so you can use smaller ones, which may enhance the appearance of the scene.

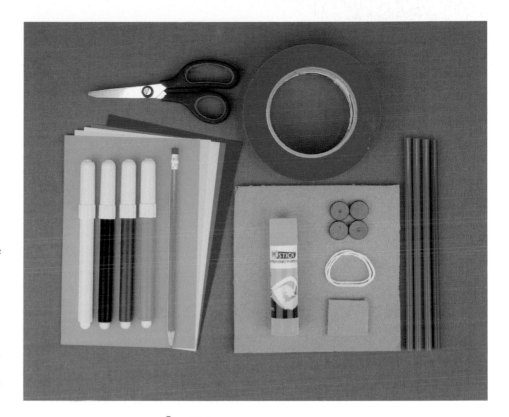

PREP

Cut the cardboard.
Young makers will need help cutting the cardboard to 6" × 6" (15 × 15 cm). Older kids can cut it themselves with large scissors.

You can avoid prep by buying cardboard that's already this size. Search the Internet for "cardboard pads" or "cardboard inserts." Make sure they are corrugated.

MINDSET: BE VISIONARY

1. The most important step in this project happens before you start making anything! What will your scene be about? Picture your finished scene in your mind. To help you get started, try answering these questions:

Who or what is your main character? (Your pet cat? A rocket ship?)

What will your main character be doing? (Chasing mice? Exploring outer space?)

How can your scenery interact with your main character? (Mice running away from the cat? Planets for the rocket to land on?)

Take the time to be visionary and stretch your imagination to make a unique scene that tells a clear story. My vision is a butterfly fluttering through a field and gathering nectar!

2. Do you have your clear vision?
Then let's get started! First, decide on a paper color for the background. Since my main character is in a field, I chose to use green so it looks like grass.

Trace the 6" × 6" (15 × 15 cm) cardboard square onto the paper and cut it out. Apply lots of glue onto the cardboard, and apply the paper smoothly.

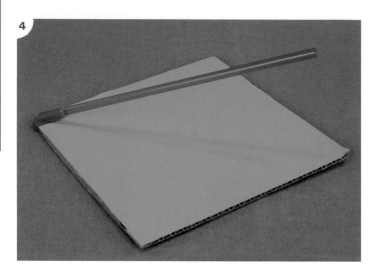

3. Time to build the pyramid!
First apply a piece of tape to the end of the straw. Leave about half of the tape hanging off.

4. Wrap the tape under a corner of the cardboard.

5. Repeat on two more corners, then tape all the straws together at the top. The pyramid is done!

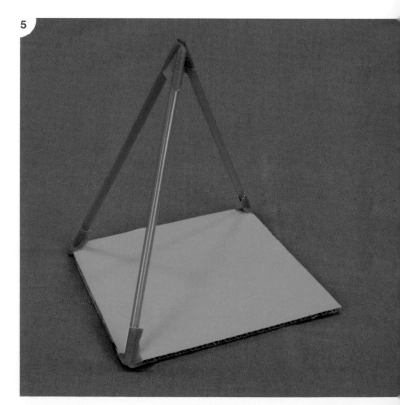

6. Now it's time to make your main character! The easiest way to make a character is to find a picture that you like and draw it using simple shapes like circles, squares, and ovals.

7. Make one or two practice drawings with pencil. When you have one you like, trace it with a colorful marker, and decorate it (like adding cat ears or rocket flames).

When you're finished, cut it out! If you have extra decorative materials, like pipe cleaners or sequins, get creative and add those to really bring your character to life.

<u>Note:</u> These next steps will help your character stay level while hanging from the string. Without these steps, your character will tilt to the side when you add the magnets.

8. Cut out a small scrap of cardboard and tape it to the back of your character.

9. Use the sharpened pencil to poke a hole in the middle of your character. Don't worry—no butterflies were harmed!

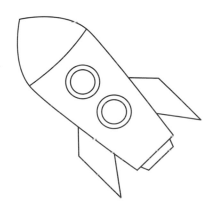

10. Cut a straw to about 4" (10 cm), and push it all the way through the hole.

11. Put the string through the straw and tape the end to the underside of your character.

12. Tape a magnet onto the underside of your character. Try to place the magnet as close to the straw as possible.

13. Tape the string to the top of the pyramid so your character hovers about 1" (2.5 cm) above the cardboard.

KNOWLEDGE: CONCEPTS AND FACTS

How do magnets work? Everything is made of atoms—very, very tiny bits of matter. Imagine a puzzle where each puzzle piece is an identical atom. By itself, an atom, like one puzzle piece, doesn't look like much, but when you clump a lot of them together they create bigger things!

Some atoms have a tiny magnetic field. Every magnetic field has a north pole and a south pole. If all of the atoms line up with their north poles pointing in the same direction and the south poles pointing the other direction, you get a magnetic force! So the magnets like the ones used in this project have all of their atoms lined up along their magnetic poles.

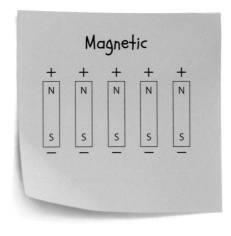

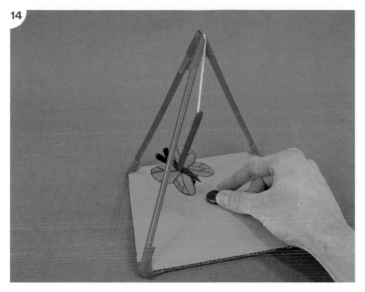

14. Time to bring your scene to life!
Place a magnet on the cardboard and push it close to your character. If your character is pulled toward the magnet, that means the north and south poles are closest, which creates magnetic attraction. We want magnetic repulsion, where the magnets push each other away. Flip the magnet over so that the magnets push each other. Your character should be invisibly pushed around, just like in the picture.

15. Tape at least three magnets onto your scene. Make sure each one is pushing against your character.

PROCESS: EVALUATE AND REDESIGN

16. Test the position of the magnets by giving your character a push. It should jitter energetically around your scene. You'll be surprised at how the placement of the magnets changes the way your character moves. Move the magnets to create different effects. What happens if they're all clumped near the middle? What happens if you spread them out? What happens if you move them all to one side? In my example, I found that evenly spacing the magnets makes the butterfly look like it's flitting from one flower to the next.

17. Finish decorating your scene by covering the magnets with paper scenery that you've decorated. Your magnetic scene is done! Now show it off and tell your audience about your character's story.

CRAFT STICK BOW

A Camp Galileo favorite, this bow is inspired by the way many real bows work and is built simply with overlapping craft sticks. I'll show you how to make a strong bow, but your challenge will be to test, evaluate, and redesign multiple arrows. Why? The design of your arrows is just as important as the bow. You'll need to innovate an arrow that's just the right size and weight!

DESIGN CHALLENGE

- Build a bow that's strong and doesn't crack or break.
- Build at least three different arrows and find the one that works best.

TOOLS AND MATERIALS

- » *Twenty or more 6" or 8" (15 or 20 cm) jumbo craft sticks*
- » *Masking tape*
- » *Notched skill sticks*
- » *Cotton string*
- » *Various plastic straws*
- » *4" (10 cm) mini hot glue sticks*
- » *Scissors*

Material substitutions

Notched skill sticks: You can use regular 4½" (11.5 cm) craft sticks, but the string may slip. Wrap the string tightly and use small pieces of tape to prevent it from unwinding.

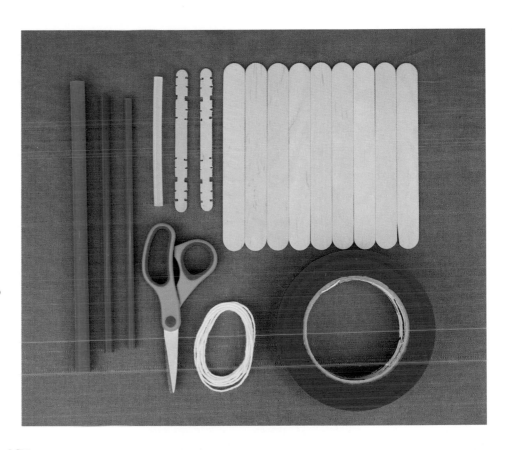

KNOWLEDGE: SKILLS AND TECHNIQUES

The key building technique in this project is to overlap and wrap. Be sure to generously overlap the jumbo craft sticks and tightly wrap them with masking tape in at least two places.

1. Start the bow. Overlap and wrap 2 jumbo craft sticks to get going.

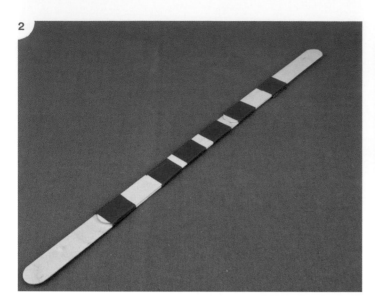

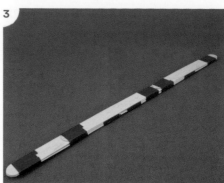

3. Make the bow stronger!
Continue overlapping and wrapping sticks on top of the row. A thick bow is a strong bow. Make sure the ends of the bow are at least two sticks thick.

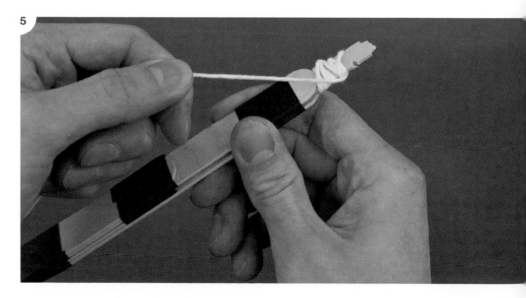

2. Make the bow longer by continuing to overlap and wrap. The more you overlap, the stronger the bow will be.

A longer bow can be more powerful, but it's also harder to make it strong enough. A bow that's about 2½ or 3 sticks long is a good length to start with.

4. Insert a skill stick in the gap at one end of your bow. Break it so just 1" (2.5 cm) sticks out. Repeat at the other end.

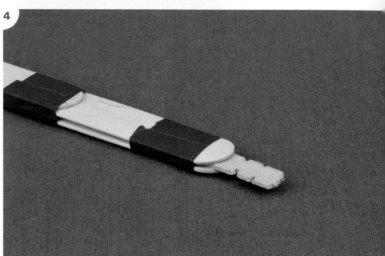

5. Cut a piece of string about twice as long as your bow. Tightly wrap the string around the skill stick many times at one end. The friction from the wrapping will keep the string in place, but if it starts to unravel, apply a small piece of tape to hold it in place.

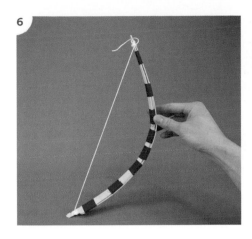

6. Test the strength of your bow. Do this with a buddy. One person will slowly and carefully bend the bow. If you hear a cracking noise, stop right away! Fix the weak area by overlapping and wrapping at least 3 sticks over the break. If your bow is strong enough, wrap the string around the skill stick inserted in the other end while your buddy holds the bow in a bent shape. Put a little piece of tape over the string if it starts to unravel.

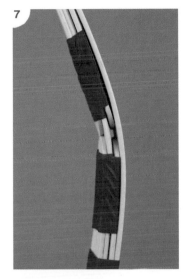

7. Before firing, take the time to evaluate your bow one more time. Look for weak spots. In my bow, I found one area that looked really thick, but was actually only two stick layers thick.

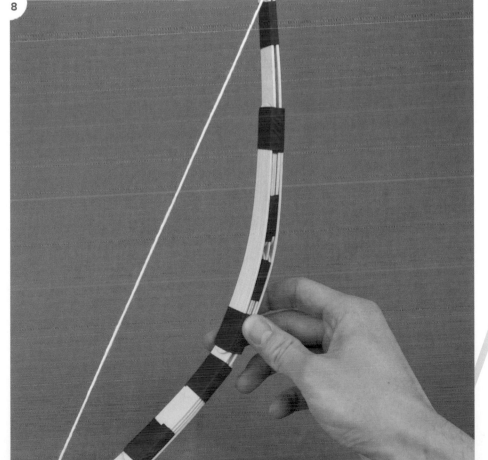

8. Now redesign.
I added another stick to cover the weak area. Does your bow need any more tinkering?

Once you're satisfied with the strength of your bow, undo the string while you make your arrows. If you keep the bow under tension for a very long time, it might lose its strength, or even break.

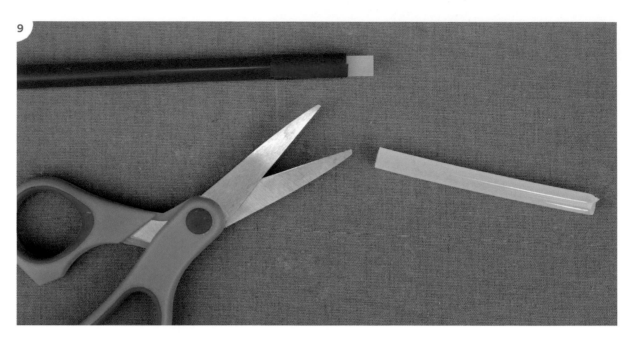

9. Time to make some arrows!
Cut a small piece of glue stick and tape it to the tip of a plastic straw.

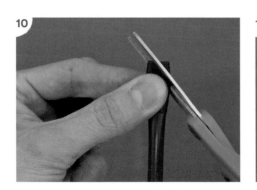

10. Create the nock. The nock is the little notch at the end of an arrow that helps it stay on the bowstring when you're firing. Start by wrapping tape around the other end of the straw from the glue stick piece. Pinch it, and use the scissors to cut off the corners.

KNOWLEDGE: CONCEPTS AND FACTS—MASS AND MOMENTUM

Have you ever tried throwing a plastic straw? It doesn't go very far. That's because a straw is not very heavy, so the air drags on it and slows it down. We need to add a little weight, or mass, to the straw. When mass is moving, it has momentum, which is a force that helps it keep going in the direction you've thrown it. In this project, the weight of the glue stick helps the plastic-straw arrow push through the air without getting slowed down.

11. Get ready to fire!
Fit the nock onto the bowstring. Make sure the arrow is in the middle of the bowstring and pointing straight forward.

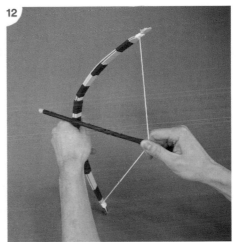

12. Are you left-handed or right-handed? Use your non-dominant hand to grip the bow, and your dominant hand to pinch the arrow. Pull back and fire by simply letting go of the arrow! No need to push the bow forward.

PROCESS: EVALUATE AND REDESIGN

13. The way to come up with the best design is to make many different types of arrows. Take the time to test and evaluate each new arrow you create. Make sure you are firing with the same amount of power and pointing the bow at the same angle. Then evaluate the arrow's performance. If your heaviest arrow works best, try making one that's even heavier at the tip! If your shortest or longest arrow is best, try making one even shorter or longer. Use this iterative process to design an arrow that really soars!

MINDSET: BE REFLECTIVE

14. Did you know that the design of the arrow is just as important as the design of the bow? Your first arrow probably isn't your best design. Try creating multiple arrows. When you find an arrow that works well, ask yourself, "What's different about this arrow that makes it better?" By looking closely at each successful arrow, and making a thoughtful guess about why it's so good, you can make even better ones.

DESIGN CHALLENGE

Create three kaleidoscope patterns that represent different feelings or emotions.

KALEIDOSCOPE

You may have seen cheap toy kaleidoscopes that have one boring pattern that repeats over and over. You know what? You can do better! Create your own kaleidoscope from scratch, and, best of all, make as many different patterns as you'd like! But keep in mind: making random patterns might not give you the best results. Put on your visionary goggles to create bold, colorful patterns inspired by feelings or emotions like happiness, excitement, and surprise.

TOOLS AND MATERIALS

- » Corrugated cardboard
- » Masking tape
- » Sharpened pencil
- » Scissors
- » 6" × ¼" (15 × 6 mm) dowel
- » Hot glue gun and glue sticks
- » Six 3" × 3" (7.5 × 7.5 cm) mirrors
- » Craft foam
- » Plastic straw that's wider than ¼" (6 mm)
- » White paper
- » Colorful markers

Material substitutions

Mirrors: craft stores and some home improvement stores sell small mirrors. Yours don't need to be exactly 3" × 3" (7.5 × 7.5 cm). In fact, rectangular mirrors would be better, but they're a little harder to find.

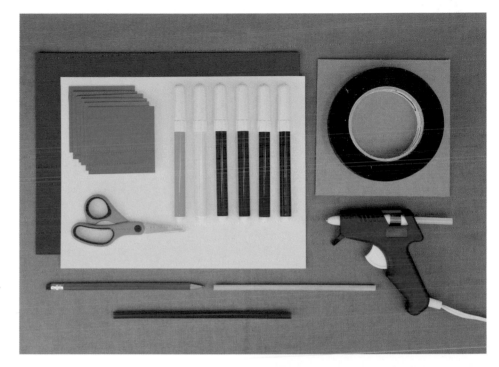

PREP

Create the Spinner

Using a full roll of masking tape as a template, trace a circle onto a scrap of cardboard, and cut it out. Hot glue the dowel to the approximate center; it doesn't need to be exact.

Tip: If you're prepping more than a few of these, I recommend buying 6" (15 cm) cardboard cake circles. They cost a little more, but they'll save you from getting sore scissor hands!

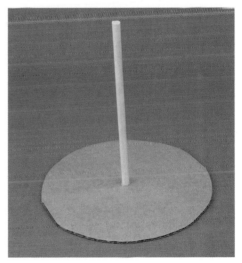

1. Let's start with the kaleidoscope prism. Line up three of the mirrors on a clean surface, reflective side down. Space them slightly apart, as shown, so the edges don't rub against each other. Tape them together.

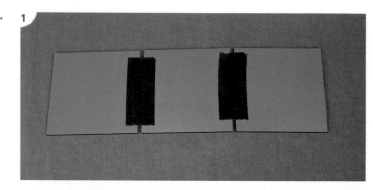

2. Fold the mirrors into a triangle and tape the last edges together. If you're using square mirrors like my example, repeat one more time.

3. Line up the two mirror prisms, and tape them together on all three sides.

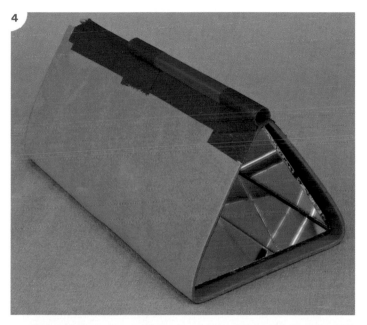

4. Wrap the prism.

Cut a sheet of craft foam a little bit wider than your mirrors. Tape one end of the foam to the mirrors, wrap it around the mirrors, and then tape down the other end to create a soft enclosure. This makes the kaleidoscope comfortable to hold and gives the mirrors a little protection from hard surfaces. Cut a straw in half and tape it to the prism. This is where the spinner will go.

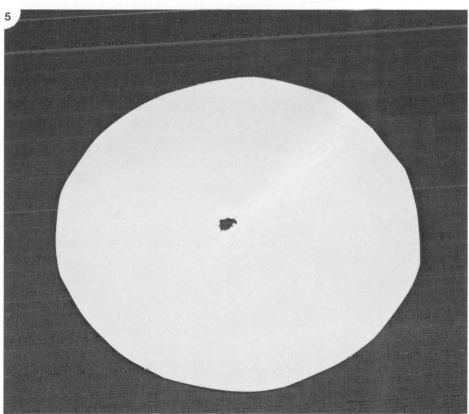

5. Time to make the patterned circles!

Using a full roll of masking tape as a template, use a pencil to trace a circle onto a sheet of white paper. Cut it out. Use a sharpened pencil to poke a hole in the middle of the circle. You don't need to find the exact center.

MINDSET: BE VISIONARY

6. Although it can be fun to create and test random squiggles, innovators always start with a vision of what they want to create. Be visionary by imagining what it will look and feel like to view into your kaleidoscope. What type of mood or emotion do you want to evoke? What kaleidoscope can you imagine that doesn't yet exist?

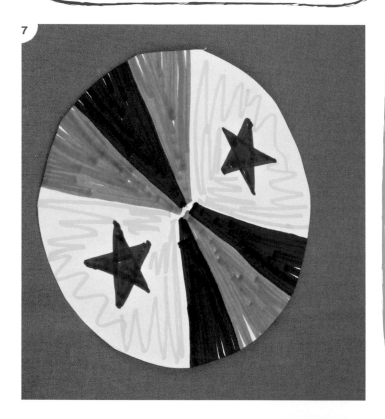

PROCESS: GENERATE IDEAS

7. Make your vision a reality by coming up with different ways to use colors and shapes to represent a specific mood or emotion.

Think of a feeling or emotion that inspires you. Happiness? Excitement? Surprise? I chose the feeling of confidence.

Think of colors that remind you of the feeling you chose. In my example, I thought blue and orange were a bold combination that made me think of confidence.

Think of shapes that remind you of your emotion. Excitement might look like lines radiating from a central point, like the sun. Confusion might look like squiggly mixed-up shapes. For my design, I thought that bold-looking triangles and stars had the feeling of confidence.

Combine your ideas to create a design that matches your vision.

8. Time to test your kaleidoscope. Slip your pattern onto the spinner and put the dowel into the straw. Leave a ½" to 1" (13 to 25 mm) space between the paper and the prism so that light can shine on the pattern.

9. Hold your kaleidoscope up to your eye. Look inside and turn the spinner. The patterns will look totally different than they do on the paper!

9

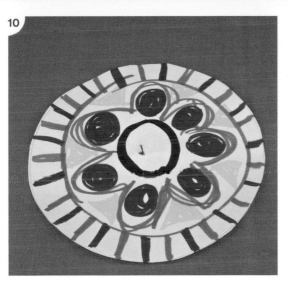

10

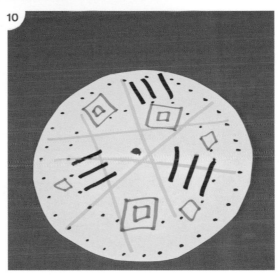

10

10. Repeat step 8 two more times, each time using a different emotion for inspiration.
When you're done, think of other things you can look at with your kaleidoscope. What happens if you look at everyday things, like a patterned shirt or a picture book? What if you create another pattern using paint, or glitter-glue, or other interesting materials? What if you tape the patterns that you drew onto a window and then look at them? Keep on innovating!

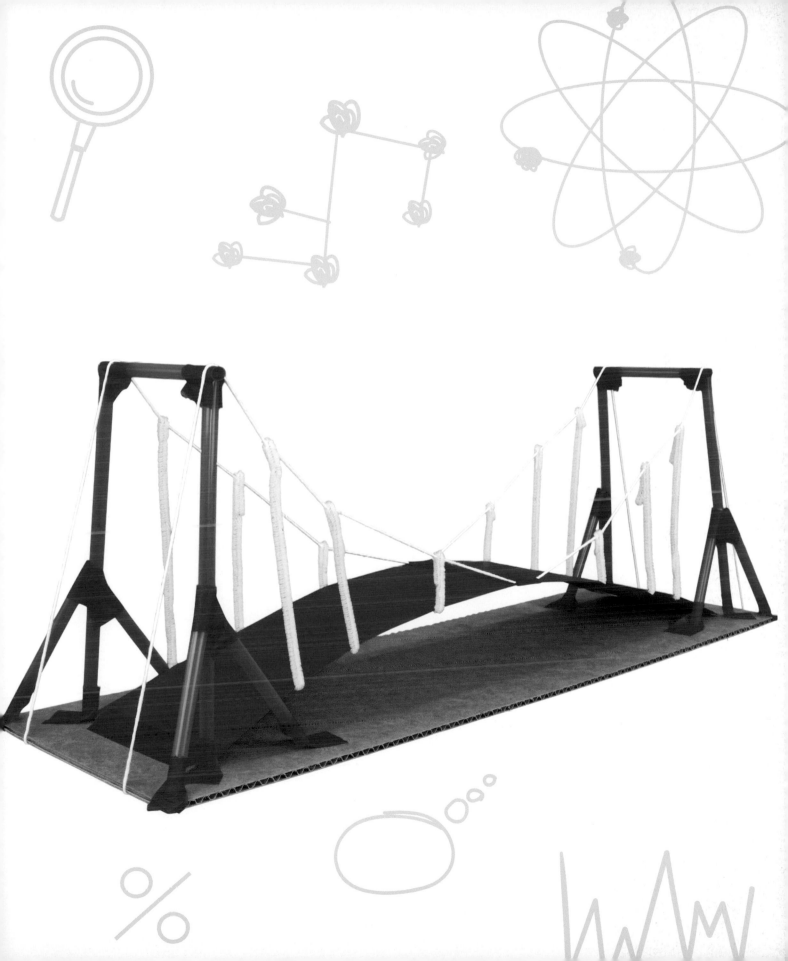

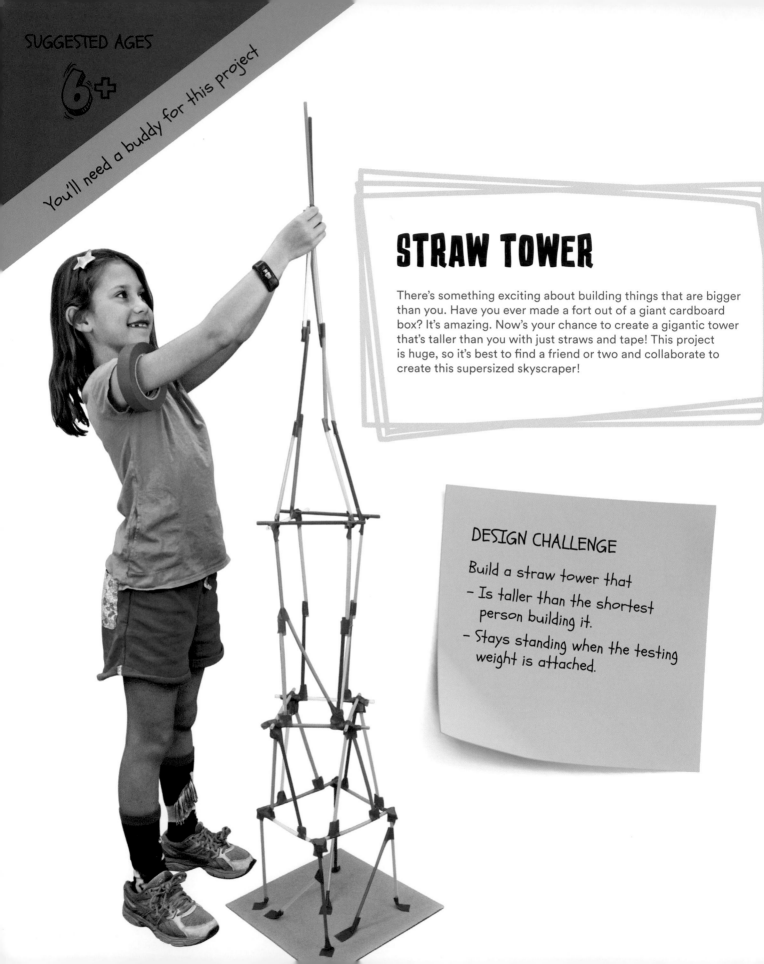

STRAW TOWER

There's something exciting about building things that are bigger than you. Have you ever made a fort out of a giant cardboard box? It's amazing. Now's your chance to create a gigantic tower that's taller than you with just straws and tape! This project is huge, so it's best to find a friend or two and collaborate to create this supersized skyscraper!

DESIGN CHALLENGE

Build a straw tower that
- Is taller than the shortest person building it.
- Stays standing when the testing weight is attached.

TOOLS AND MATERIALS

» *Small binder clip*
» *Two or more metal washers*
» *Masking tape*
» *Lots of non-bendy straws*
» *12" × 12" (30 × 30 cm) corrugated
   cardboard*

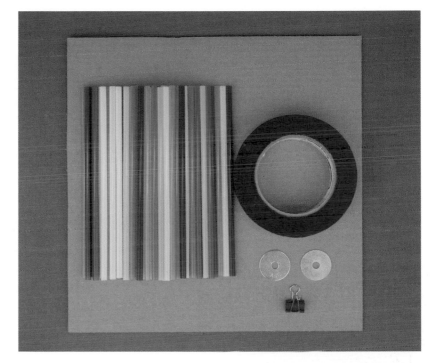

PREP

Cut the cardboard
Cutting pieces of cardboard can be
tough for young kids. An adult may need
to cut out the base. It doesn't need to be
precisely 12" × 12" (30 × 30 cm).

Make the testing weight
Prep the testing weight by taping at least
two large washers to a binder clip. Two
large washers present a relatively easy
challenge. You can adjust the difficulty of
the challenge by adding more weight.

KNOWLEDGE: SKILLS AND TECHNIQUES

Good connections are key for a strong tower, and taping straws at different angles can be tricky. Before getting started, take a look at these straw-building techniques.

Uprights—Tape the straw to the cardboard so half the tape is pressed flat against the cardboard and the other half is pinched around the straw.

Wraparounds—When connecting two straws together, wrap the tape completely around one of the straws and stick the tape to itself.

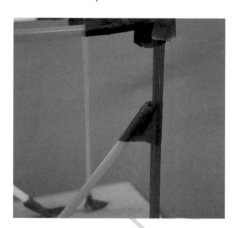

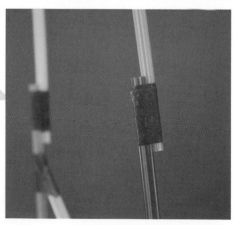

Overlap and wrap—To make a long beam, overlap two straws by about 1" (2.5 cm). Then tightly wrap a piece of tape around it.

1. Start building!
Place half a piece of tape on a straw; leave the other half hanging off.

2. Use the upright-construction technique to start your tower. I started with just four, but additional uprights might make the structure even more stable.

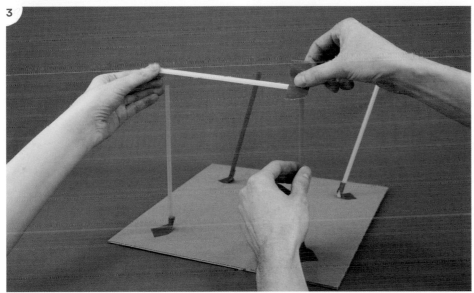

PROCESS: CREATE

3. Building a tower is a big job, and it's tough to do it alone. A fun way to share the challenge is to take turns with two important jobs: The builder and the architect. The architect decides where to put the next straw and holds it in place. The builder gets the tape and attaches the straws. After a straw is attached, switch roles so everyone gets to come up with ideas and do some building.

MINDSET: BE COLLABORATIVE

4. As you're building, you might think that your ideas and the way you build are the best, but remember: You're working with a partner who also has great thoughts and amazing skills! Be collaborative by listening to your partner's ideas, sharing your thoughts, and working together toward a common goal. Your partner will likely have lots of great ideas you wouldn't have thought of on your own. Build on each other's ideas to take your tower to new heights!

5. Keep building!
It looks strong, right? But if you put a little weight on it, it leans over. We need a new building technique.

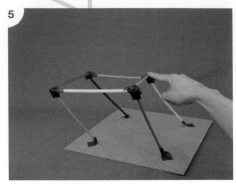

6. The answer: trusses!
These are triangles that are used in engineering to make corners and square shapes stronger. Use trusses throughout your structure, especially whenever you see a square shape that's bending.

KNOWLEDGE: CONCEPTS AND FACTS ABOUT TRUSSES

The triangle is a strong and useful shape in engineering. Triangles are strong shapes because they don't bend or collapse when they hold up weight. On the other hand, rectangles can easily collapse into flattened parallelograms if you put too much weight on them. When engineers use triangles to make a structure stronger, it's called a truss. Use plenty of trusses to make your tower stand strong!

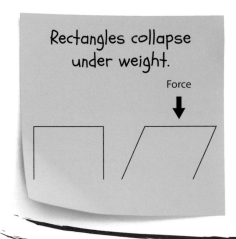

Rectangles collapse under weight.

Force

Triangles hold their shape.

Force

7. Build it taller!
This tower is two straws tall

8. Each time the tower gets one straw length taller, it's time to test! Clip the testing weight you made earlier onto the top of the tower in at least two places. If the tower remains standing, build it taller! If it falls over, build it stronger before adding any more height.

9. Continue sharing the architect and builder roles and testing each time the tower becomes one straw length taller.

Near the top, you can add a spire to quickly add a lot of height!

Once your tower is taller than the shortest person on your building team, you've succeeded! Give your collaborators a hearty high five!

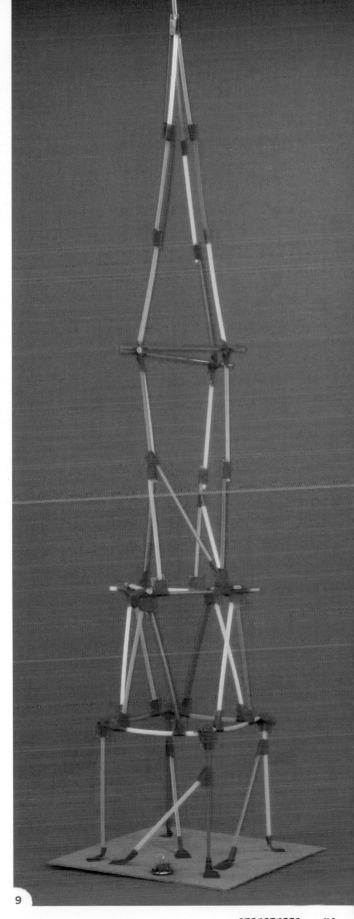

SUSPENSION BRIDGE

Modern suspension bridges are a feat of engineering! The bridge deck—the part that people and vehicles travel on—is suspended from thick metal cables, which in turn are supported by tall towers. This project uses the same principles as a real suspension bridge, except all you need is some paper, cardboard, string, and straws! This is a big project, but with a little determination, you'll have a strong and sturdy structure!

DESIGN CHALLENGE

Build a suspension bridge that
- Has two stable towers
- Can hold weight anywhere on the deck without sagging.

TOOLS AND MATERIALS

- » *Small cup*
- » *Coins or washers*
- » *Pipe cleaners*
- » *Masking tape*
- » *Card stock*
- » *Scissors*
- » *6" × 24" (15 × 61 cm) piece of corrugated cardboard*
- » *Plastic straws*
- » *Cotton string*

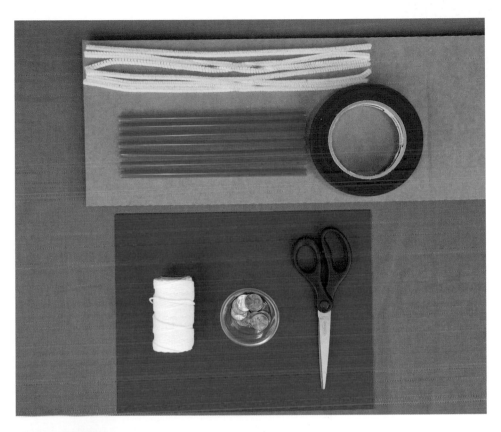

PREP

Cut the cardboard
An adult will need to cut a 6" × 24" (15 × 61 cm) piece of cardboard. It doesn't have to be precisely that size. Use a box cutter and a cutting mat to speed up this prep.

Create a testing weight
Fill a small lightweight cup with 10 coins or metal washers. Fold a pipe cleaner in half and tape the ends to opposite sides of the cup.

1. Start by creating the bridge deck. Fold a piece of card stock in half lengthwise. Cut it in half along that folded line. Overlap the two pieces by 1" (2.5 cm) or so and tape the two pieces together on top and underneath to make a long strip of paper.

2. Tape one end of the deck 1" (2.5 cm) or so from one end of the cardboard. Raise the middle of the deck up to 3" (7.5 cm) above the cardboard. Tape the other end down.

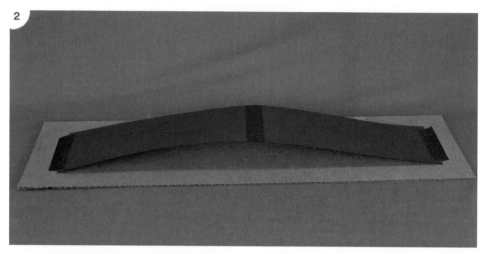

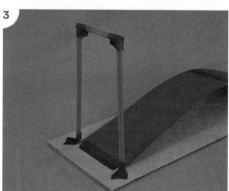

3. Time to build the towers.

The towers are the parts that will actually support the weight that's placed on the bridge, so they have to be strong and stable. Use the taping techniques shown in the Knowledge: Skills and Techniques section of the Straw Tower project (page 38). Start by taping two whole straws onto the cardboard near the corners of the deck. Cut and tape another short straw piece to connect the tops of the long straws.

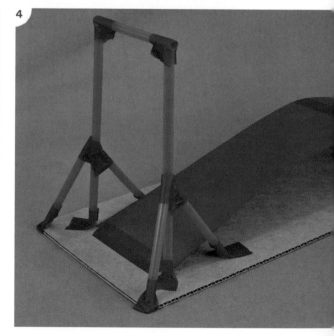

4. Make it strong and stable!

Since this is part of your design challenge, it's up to you to figure out the best way to do this.

<u>Hint:</u> Remember to use trusses. See the Knowledge: Concepts and Facts about Trusses section of the Straw Tower project for more information (page 40).

PROCESS: TEST, EVALUATE, AND REDESIGN

5. Test your tower's strength and stability by hanging your test weight from the top bar. Tilt the cardboard. Does the tower lean with the weight? Does the tape come loose? Give the cardboard a shake. If your tower doesn't budge, you're ready to move on!

If your tower bends, look carefully to find a weak spot. Check the tape connections and strengthen if needed. Keep adding more trusses to the main tower, testing and redesigning until the tower stops wobbling.

5

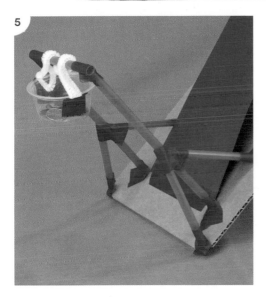

7

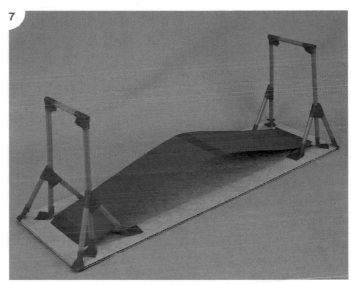

7. Once you've discovered a successful design, copy it on the other side of the deck.

MINDSET: BE DETERMINED

6. Be determined and redesign your tower until it's strong and stable. If you're feeling frustrated, try something radically different or take a short break and come back to the tower with fresh eyes. Innovators persevere until they reach their goals, and a stable tower design will ensure that the rest of the bridge is strong.

8

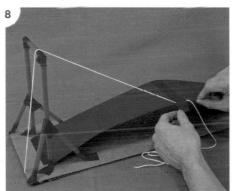

8. Create the main cable!
Cut a piece of string to about 36" (91 cm) and tape one end to the underside of the cardboard. Drape it over the top of your tower and, while pulling the string taut, but not too tight, tape it to the middle of the deck. If the string slips off the tower, apply a small piece of tape to hold it in place. Drape the string over the other tower and tape the other end of the string to the underside of the cardboard.

9

9. Repeat step 8 on the other side of the deck and towers so that you have two main cables!

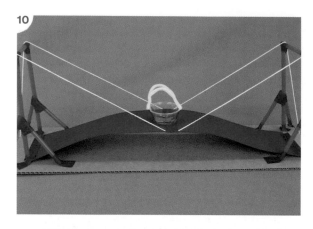

10. Test the bridge's suspension! Place the weight in the middle of the bridge. Amazing—the deck holds it up! But notice: If you move the weight off to the side, the deck sags quite a bit.

Tip: If the testing weight slides off the paper, use a small tape loop on the underside of the cup to hold it in place.

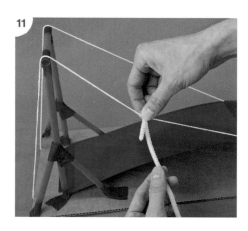

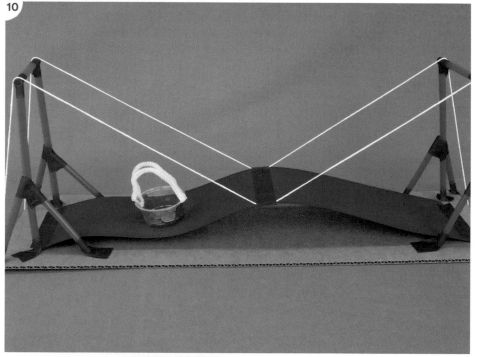

11. To support the entire span of the bridge, you'll need to create suspension cables that connect the main cable to the deck. Start by folding and tightly pinching a pipe cleaner around the main cable. Pinch it tightly so it grips onto the string and doesn't slide. If you have a hard time with it, use a small piece of tape to keep it in place.

12. Find the spot where the pipe cleaner meets the deck, and bend it into an L shape. Avoid pulling on the main cable or you might put too much tension on it! Cut the pipe cleaner so the bottom of the L is about 1" (2.5 cm) long. Tape it to the underside of the deck.

13. Repeat on the other side and then test! Each time you add a pair of suspension cables, place the testing weight on the deck. Notice that the deck no longer sags where the cables are, but it still needs improvement just to the right of that spot.

MINDSET: BE DETERMINED

14. Keep going! Be determined and create as many sets of suspension cables as you need. If the going gets tough, take a break and roll a car across your bridge, or draw some water underneath it. Once you're rejuvenated, finish up the cables, and you'll have a suspension bridge that can hold weight anywhere along the deck!

3

HOUSEHOLD INNOVATIONS

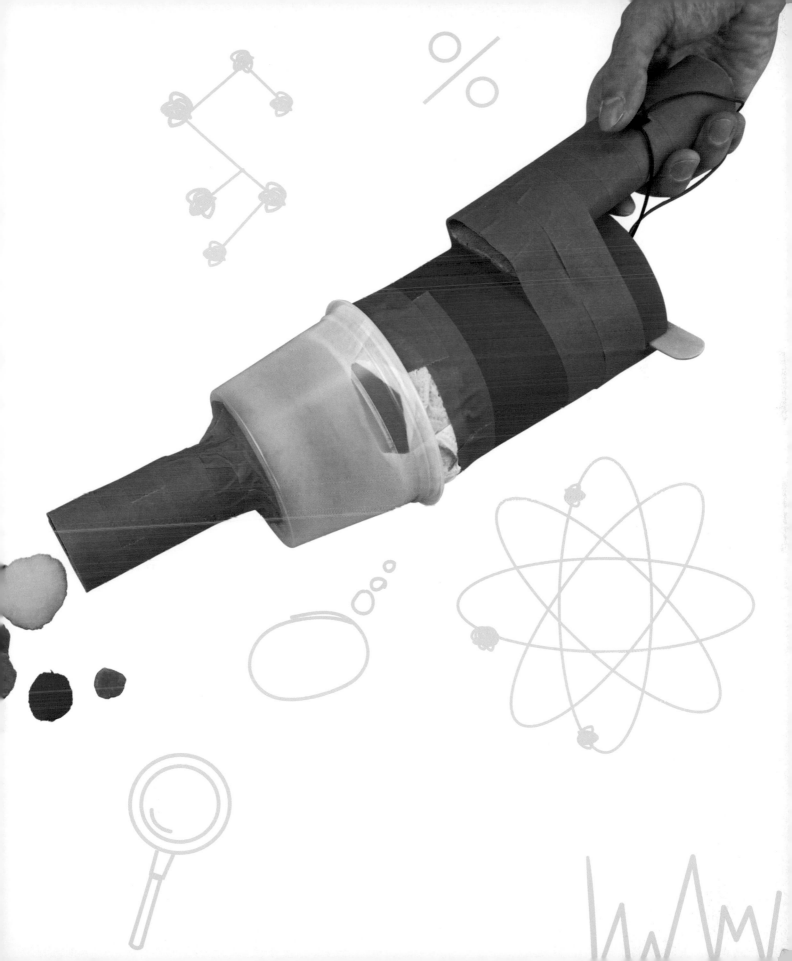

GRABBER

Have you ever dropped something behind the sofa that you couldn't get hold of? Or maybe your parents keep the best snacks on the top shelf, out of reach? Well then, this project is for you! This grabber will extend your reach by over 30" (76 cm)! I'll show you how to make a basic grabber, and then it's up to you to improve its grip. You can thank me later when you grab that package of cookies from the top of the fridge.

DESIGN CHALLENGE

Build a grabber that can pick up three to five different types of objects with ease.

TOOLS AND MATERIALS

- » Clean, unbent corrugated cardboard
- » 2 paint stirrers
- » Ruler
- » Scissors
- » Sharpened pencil
- » Masking tape
- » 1½" (3.8 cm) brass paper fasteners
- » ⅛" × 3½" (3 mm × 9 cm) rubber band
- » String
- » Craft sticks, foam, paperclips, or other materials for improving the grabber's grip
- » Assorted objects to pick up

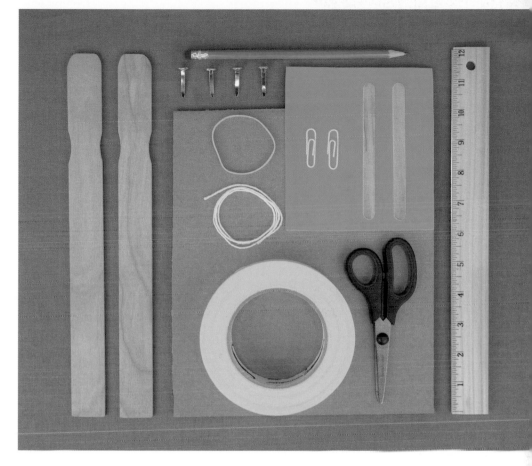

PREP

Cut the cardboard

Cutting cardboard with scissors is difficult for kids under the age of 8 or 9. Adults might need to prep steps 2 to 4. If so, you can speed up the process by using a utility knife and cutting mat, or a paper cutter.

1. Make the handle.

Overlap the paint stirrers by about 4" (10 cm), and wrap them tightly with masking tape in at least two places.

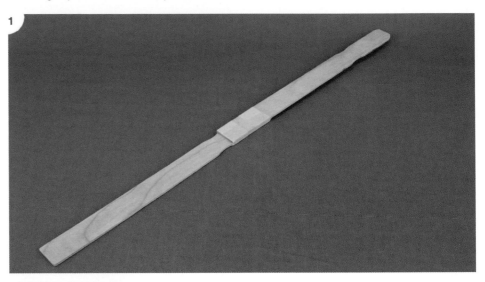

2. Cut the cardboard.

Cut three pieces of cardboard that are about 10" (25.5 cm) long and 1½" (3.8 cm) wide, and two pieces that are 5" (12.5 cm) long and 1½" (3.8 cm) wide. If you are doing this with scissors, it's easiest to first score the cutting line with an open scissor blade, then cut along the same line, using the scissors normally.

Tip: For the strongest grabber possible, be sure to cut along (not across) the corrugations as shown.

3. Set out your five pieces.
Use a sharpened pencil to poke hinge holes in the cardboard as shown. Note that one piece isn't poked at all. Keep your pencil sharp by placing a scrap piece of cardboard behind the area you're piercing.

The holes should be at least ½" (1.25 cm) from the edges. They don't need to be very big.

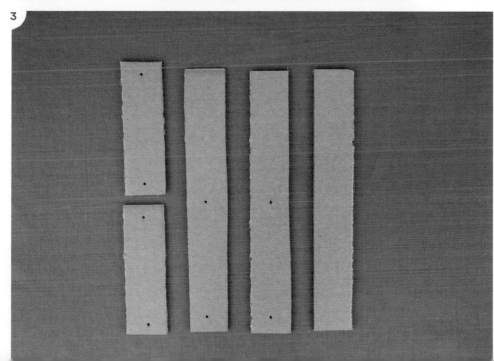

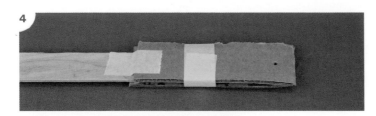

4. Take the piece that doesn't have holes, fold it in half, and tape it to the end of the handle as shown. About 1" (2.5 cm) of the folded cardboard should extend beyond the wooden handle. Poke a hole through that part of the cardboard.

5. Center the two remaining 10" (25.5 cm) pieces of cardboard, as shown, over the hole you just poked. Insert a paper fastener through the lined-up holes in the middle. Flip the piece over carefully and fold the fastener tabs completely flat. Secure the tabs in place with tape.

This step is important. If the fastener tabs are not folded and taped, the grabber will come undone.

6. Attach the two 5" (12.5 cm) pieces with paper fasteners as shown. Again, fold and tape the fastener tabs.

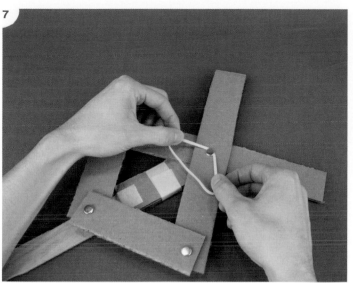

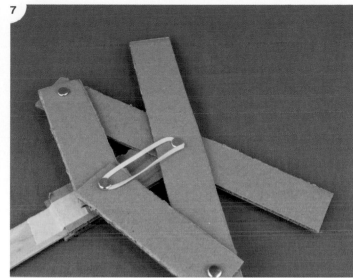

7. Attach the rubber band.
This will allow the grabber to open automatically. Stretch the rubber band with both hands and slip it under one of the middle fasteners as shown. Repeat with the other middle fastener.

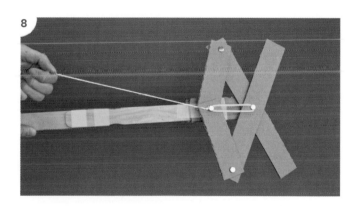

8. Tie a piece of string to the fastener as shown.
The grabber is ready to test! Give the string a tug: Your grabber should close.

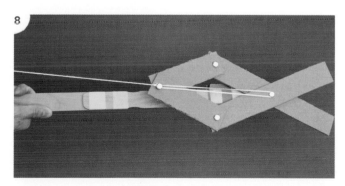

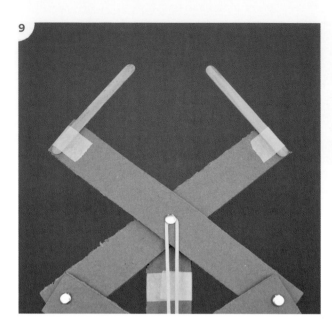

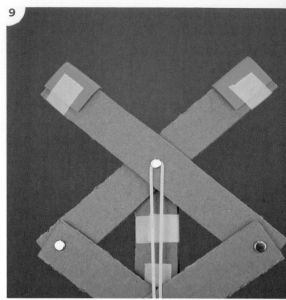

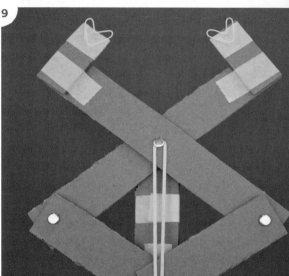

PROCESS: CREATE AND TEST

9. Time to start innovating.
Your grabber mechanism is done, but it probably isn't very good at picking things up yet. That's because the cardboard surface is slippery: You'll need to improve its grip. Test the various materials you've gathered to figure out which provides your grabber with the best grip by cutting and attaching the materials to your grabber's pinchers with tape.

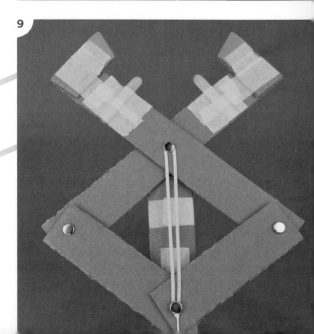

MINDSET: BE DETERMINED

10. Find three to five objects of different shapes, weights, and sizes—such as a marble, a cup, or a paper tube. Don't settle for a grabber that works just sometimes. Take apart your first grip design and keep trying new things until your grabber can pick up just about anything with ease!

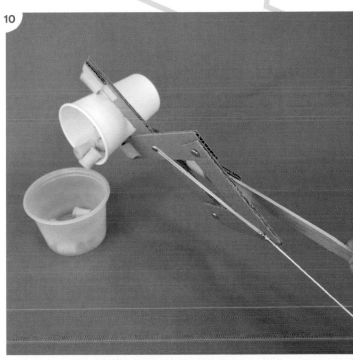

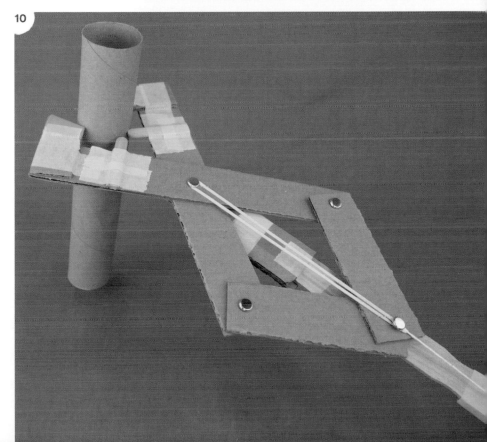

Tip: Creative Constraints
Parents and teachers: Limit the number of materials you hand out for improving the grabber. Assign a specific number of materials per child, such as two craft sticks, one small piece of cardboard, and one small rectangle of foam. Limiting the materials prompts children to use their resources more creatively. Otherwise, they may try to solve their problems by simply adding on more and more materials.

DESIGN CHALLENGE

Build a vacuum that

- Can suck up all sizes of pom-poms

- Prevents the smallest pom-poms from passing through the filter

HANDHELD VACUUM

When I say, "You'll make a vacuum cleaner," I mean a real one! This project works just like a vacuum that you can buy at the store. It will be up to you to create, test, and evaluate the best possible filter for your vacuum so it can clean up just about anything. For once, you'll be excited when you're asked to clean your home!

TOOLS AND MATERIALS

» *Round cardboard container about 4" (10 cm) wide*
» *Utility knife*
» *Wire strippers*
» *Paper*
» *Scissors*
» *Masking tape*
» *AA battery pack*
» *Momentary push button*
» *Small DC project motor (1.5 to 3 volts)*
» *Plastic propeller with 2 mm hole for the motor shaft*
» *6" (15 cm) jumbo craft stick*
» *Paper towels*
» *16 oz (475 ml) round plastic container*
» *Small Phillips screwdriver*
» *Paper towel tube*
» *AA batteries*
» *Assorted pom-poms*

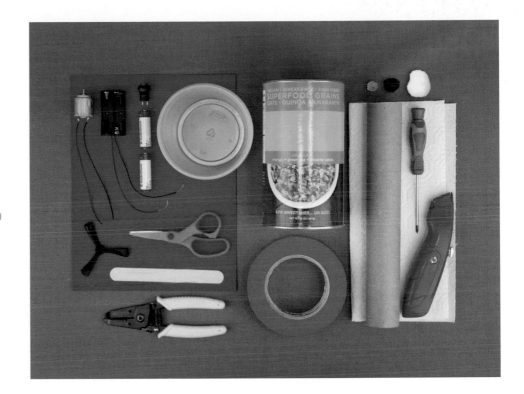

Material sources: Electronics

I acknowledge that there are some parts for this project that might be tricky to find, namely the motor, battery pack, push button, and propeller. However, this project has perhaps the greatest, "I can't believe I made that!" moment, so I've decided that the extra effort to find these materials is worth it. Here are a few tips to find the right parts online or in an electronics store:

Propeller: Search for "plastic propeller 2 mm." Find one that has at least 3 blades and specifically states that it can fit onto a 2 mm motor shaft. Make sure the propeller is less than 3" (7.5 cm) in diameter; it needs to fit inside your cardboard container.

Motor: Search for "small DC motor with wires." Find one that can spin at at least 15,000 rpm, has a 2 mm motor shaft, is rated for 1.5 to 3 volts, and comes with attached wires.

Battery pack: Search for "AA battery pack." Find one that can hold two AA batteries and has attached wires.

Push button: Search for "momentary push button."

Material sources: Containers

You can find plastic containers at delis (perhaps for free if you ask nicely!) In the U.S., the sizes are usually standardized, and the container opening should be about 4.5" (11.5 cm).

The opening in the cardboard container needs to be a little smaller than the opening of the plastic container. Containers for oats and bread crumbs are usually about right. Bring your ruler the next time you're at the grocery store!

PREP

Cut the container
An adult will need to cut off the bottom of the cardboard container with a utility knife.

Strip the wires
An adult will need to strip off about 1" (2.5 cm) of the insulation from the wires. This will make it much easier to twist the wires together. If you don't have wire strippers, you can carefully pinch the wire between scissor blades, and pull it through the scissors to remove the insulation.

1. This first step is optional, but it will make your vacuum look snappy! Cut a piece of paper to the same height as your cardboard container and long enough to wrap around it. Tape the paper in place to cover all the logos and words.

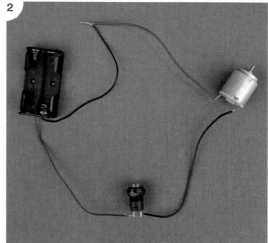

2. Make your vacuum circuit!
Twist the wires together as shown, taking care that each connection is tightly wrapped. Don't put in the batteries yet. If you do, and the exposed wires accidentally cross, you might create a short circuit, which can dangerously overheat the batteries.

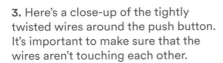

3. Here's a close-up of the tightly twisted wires around the push button. It's important to make sure that the wires aren't touching each other.

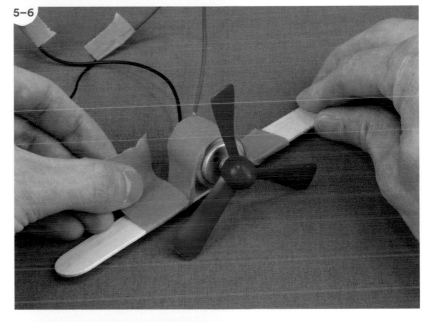

4. Pinch small pieces of tape around the wires to ensure they don't touch. Wrap a piece of tape around the wire connection between the motor and battery pack as well.

KNOWLEDGE: CONCEPTS AND FACTS

In electrical engineering, a circuit is a path for electrons to flow through. Many circuits, like this one, are circular in shape. The electrons flow from the positive side of the battery, through the motor, and back to the negative side. This is because the negative side of batteries has a lower voltage than the positive side, and electrons always move from higher to lower voltage.

If a circuit is incomplete, or open, then the electrons aren't able to flow from the higher voltage side to the lower voltage side and nothing happens. When the circuit is complete, or closed, the electrons can flow again. In the circuit for our vacuum, the push button makes it easy for you to open and close the circuit!

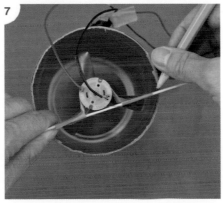

5. Fit the propeller onto the motor shaft, then tape it onto the center of the 6" (15 cm) craft stick.

6. Wrap two more pieces of tape around the stick on either side of the motor to hold it in place.

7. Position the motor so it's centered over the cut-off end of the container, and then mark the points where the stick touches the container.

8. Cut a slit in the container at the spots you marked, then slip the craft stick in. This will position the motor securely in the middle.

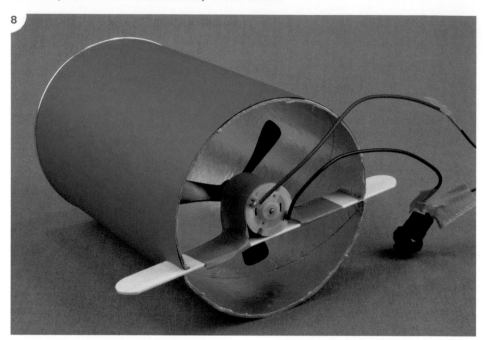

9. Install the batteries and give it a test! The suction of the fan should be able to lift a paper towel! If the fan is blowing the wrong way, flip the batteries around.

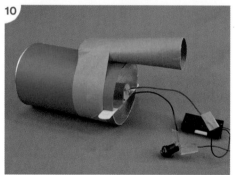

10. Right now, the vacuum is very hard to use. Create a handle by cutting the paper towel tube in half, then strapping it to the back of the vacuum with at least two long pieces of tape.

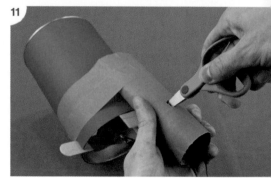

11. Use the Phillips head screwdriver to poke a hole near the middle of the handle. Widen the hole by inserting a closed pair of scissors and twisting it a few times.

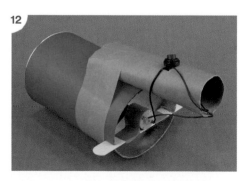

12. Fit the push button into the hole and tuck the battery pack inside the handle—now it's officially a handheld device! However, if you try to vacuum things with it, they'll get sucked into the spinning propeller! You'll need to make a collection canister and a filter.

MAKE THE CANISTER AND FILTER

1. Use the Phillips head screwdriver again to poke a hole centered in the bottom of the plastic container.

2. Use scissors to make radiating 1" (2.5 cm) cuts all the way around the hole (like pie slices).

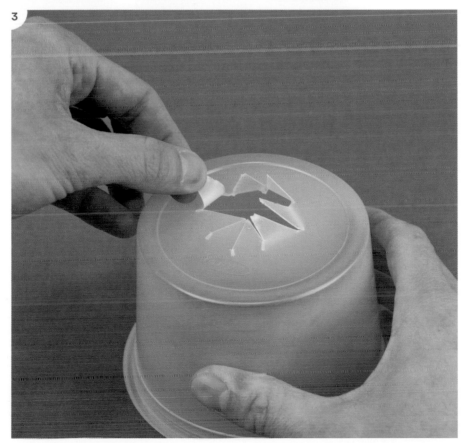

3. Working one at a time, pull each triangular cut upward. Be careful! The plastic edges might be sharp.

4. Push the second half of the paper towel tube through the hole in the container's side. Tape it to the upturned plastic cuts. Apply more tape anywhere you see a hole in the container. Optional: Cover the tube in colored tape to match the vacuum!

KNOWLEDGE: CONCEPTS AND FACTS

Vacuum filters allow air to pass through, but not dust or other debris. This is a challenge for engineers: If the holes in the filter are too small, then air can't pass through fast enough, and the vacuum loses power. However, if the holes are too big, then dust or other objects will pass through the filter and hit the motor, propeller, etc. The filter is one of the most important parts of a vacuum, so this is what you'll need to test, evaluate, and redesign the most.

5. The collection canister and nozzle are done, now it's time to make the last part: the filter! Fold a paper towel in half and cut slits or small shapes into it. This will be your filter. Don't worry if the first one isn't perfect—they're easy to create and test!

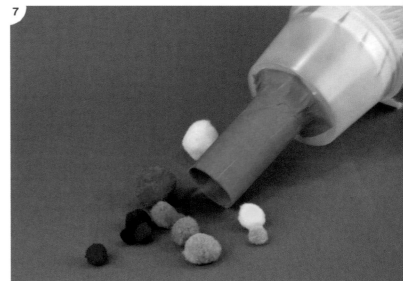

6. To install the filter, place it over the vacuum opening, and then fit the plastic container snugly over it. It should stay in place with only friction. If you wish, cut off the large parts of the paper towel that remain outside the canister.

PROCESS: TEST AND EVALUATE

7. Test it!
Try vacuuming different sized pom-poms.
Remember: The challenge for a good filter is to allow air to pass through easily while still catching the smallest things. By testing and evaluating different filter designs, you'll discover what works best and you'll be able to redesign a filter that will work even better than your first one.

MINDSET: BE REFLECTIVE

8. Playing with your freshly finished vacuum cleaner will be surprisingly fun! However, be sure to take some time to reflect and think about what is and isn't working in your filter design. Are there any holes big enough to let pom-poms through? Are the holes so small that not enough air can pass through to create suction? Think about what can be improved so you can make another filter to solve the problems you see.

10. The innovating doesn't have to stop here. What else can you do to improve your vacuum? What about making a filter from a different material that can filter out even smaller things? Hint: Loose materials like plastic mesh or burlap might work well. What if you tried a different tool—like a hole punch—to make holes in the filter? What about giving your invention a name? Like the DustZapper 3000! What about making it even more comfortable to use? Keep going!

9. Keep creating, testing, and evaluating until you have a filter that achieves the design challenge! Once you've found the best one, trim off the excess paper towel, and tape it to the vacuum.

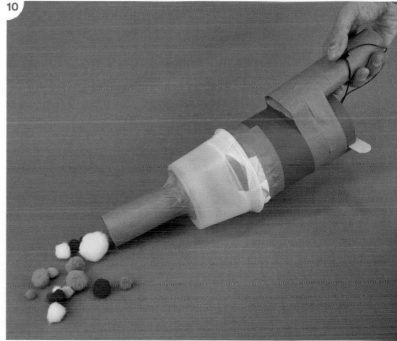

4
MACHINES

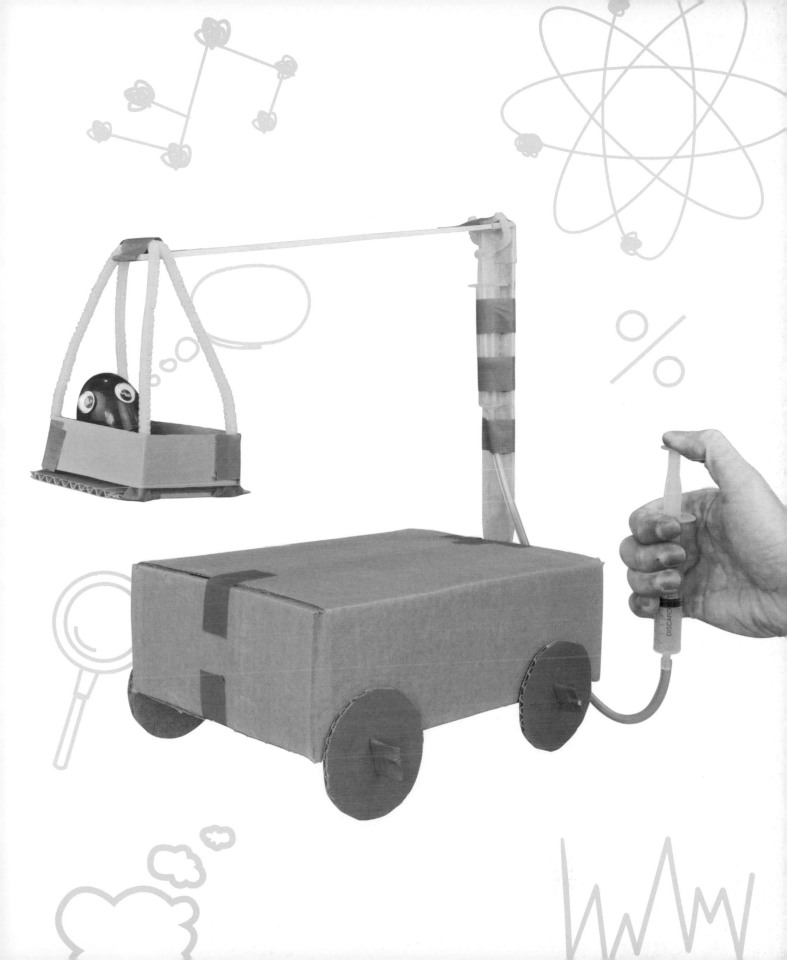

CRANE

Cranes for lifting and moving heavy objects were in use over 2,500 years ago. In the centuries since then, engineers have figured out ways to make cranes bigger, stronger, and most importantly, more stable. Preventing cranes from tipping over while carrying a heavy load is a big engineering challenge. Now you can try making your own super-stable crane!

DESIGN CHALLENGE

Build a crane that
- Doesn't tip over
- Is super strong
- Can lift the greatest possible amount of weight

TOOLS AND MATERIALS

- » ¼" (6 mm) dowel 36" long (91 cm)*
- » Masking tape
- » 10" × 12" (25 × 30 cm) piece of corrugated cardboard (or similar)*
- » Plastic straws
- » Paper clips
- » Scissors
- » Sharpened pencil
- » String
- » Small paper cup
- » Pipe cleaner
- » Metal washers (or other small weights)
- » 6" (15 cm) jumbo craft sticks

* The length of the dowel and the size of the cardboard affect how challenging this project will be. Longer dowels and smaller pieces of cardboard are more difficult to stabilize. Shorter dowels with larger cardboard are easier.

KNOWLEDGE: SKILLS AND TECHNIQUES

Holding two objects in the right position and taping them together can be tricky for young hands. Use the "half-on/half-off" taping technique (page 38) to make the process easier! First apply the tape to the objects individually so that half of each length of tape is hanging free. Then arrange and hold the two objects in the right position and secure the free ends of the tape!

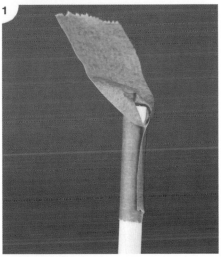

1. Use the half-on/half-off taping technique!
Apply a piece of tape onto the end of the dowel.

2. Wrap the tape under the short side of the cardboard.

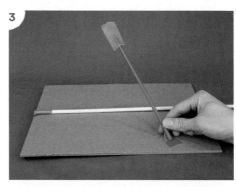

3. Make the crane stronger! Keep using the half-on/half-off taping technique to attach a straw to the cardboard. Tape the other end to the dowel.

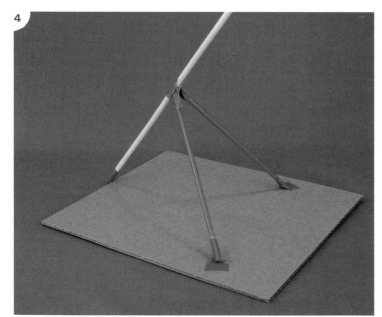

4. Position another straw directly across from the first and attach it to the cardboard and the dowel. This will give the dowel solid support.

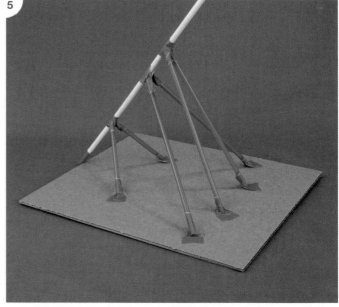

5. Add trusses to your crane's structure to help to make it strong and stable. Read about how trusses add strength to structures in step 5 of the Straw Tower project (page 40).

6. Prepare to add the string. First unbend a paper clip and tape it to the top of the dowel.

7. Make a winch for winding the string! Cut two scraps of cardboard that are about 1½" × 4" (4 × 10 cm). Bend them in half. Use a sharpened pencil to poke a hole in each one.

8. Tape the two pieces onto the cardboard base so that the holes are facing each other. Thread the pencil through the holes in each.

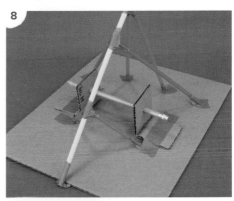

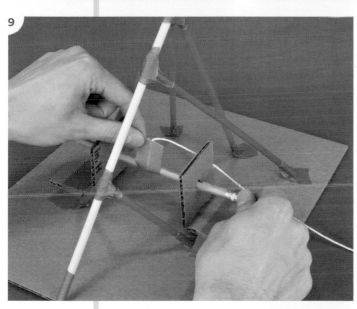

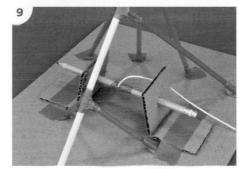

9. Use the half-on/half-off taping technique to attach a piece of string that's about twice as long as your dowel to the pencil. Turn the pencil to wrap the tape around it! Thread the opposite end of the string through the hook at the top of the dowel.

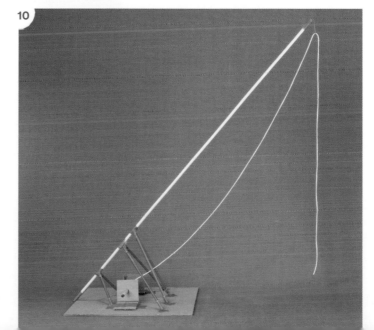

10. The crane structure is done!

IMPROVE THE CRANE

1. You'll need to attach something on the free end of the string for holding onto whatever you are lifting. In this example, I've used a simple hook made from a paper clip, but your crane could use a basket, a magnet, a net, or something else!

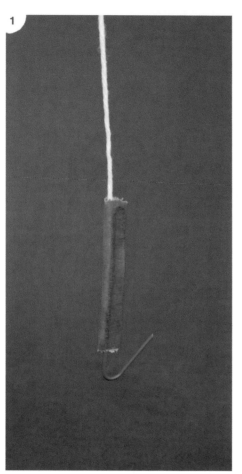

2. Create the test weight.
In this example, I've made a bucket with a small cup and a pipe cleaner, and then put metal washers in my bucket as the test load. Start with something lightweight, and add more weight after each successful test.

PROCESS: TEST AND REDESIGN

3. Hang the test weight off the hook at the end of the string. Oh no! The weight might make your crane tip over like mine. When this happens, look for ways to make your crane more stable.

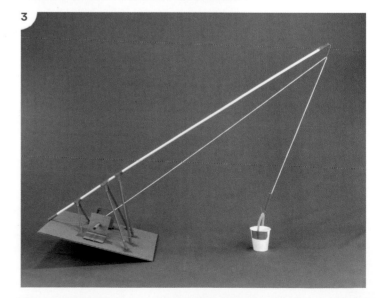

MINDSET: BE DETERMINED

4. Don't be discouraged if your crane is unstable at the start. Put in the effort to improve the crane, even in the face of failure. It might be fun to play with it as is, but think of how much better it'll be once it can hold more than just an empty paper cup. Set a weight goal and then persevere until you achieve your goal. If it comes easily, set an even harder goal.

5. One way to redesign your crane is to add extra improvements, such as outriggers (out-riggers). These are beams that help stabilize structures or vehicles. Overlap at least half of your large craft sticks with the underside of the cardboard base and tape it in at least two places.

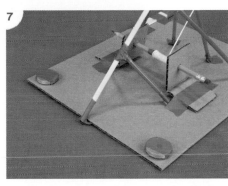

6. Lengthen the outriggers by attaching another craft stick to make your crane even more stable! Continue to overlap the sticks and tape in two or more places to make sure it doesn't bend.

7. Another way engineers stabilize cranes is by adding a counterweight. The word "counter" means "against" and counterweights help with balance by using one weight against another. So if your crane is tipping forward, add counterweights to the back!

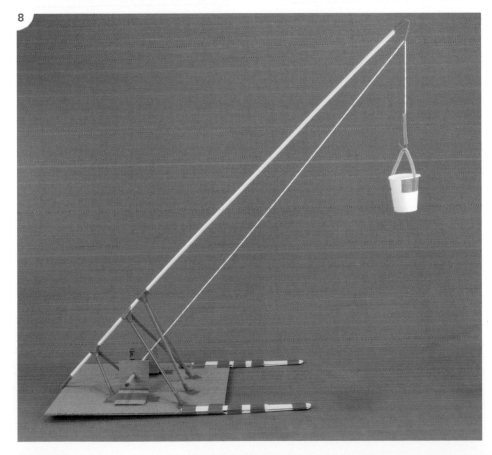

8. Success!
After each successful test, add a little more weight until your crane tips over again. You might notice here that the back of the crane is still lifting from the ground a little.

9. Those counterweights made this crane even more stable. But the innovation doesn't end here. How else can you improve your crane? Here are some questions to consider:

How can you combine outriggers and counterweights to make the crane super stable?

How can you build a crank onto your winch?

How can you redesign the crane hook so it can pick up other things, like a small stuffed animal?

DESIGN CHALLENGE

Build a pneumatic lift that

- Can raise and lower the arm by at least 12" (30 cm)

- Can raise and lower a load without it falling out

PNEUMATIC LIFT

Did you know you can lift incredibly heavy things using just air? It's true! Pneumatic (*new-mat-ik*) means powered by air pressure, and it's up to you to create a pneumatic-powered machine that can raise a load, like a plastic egg, as high as possible! You'll need to be determined to get your pneumatic machine in its best working order.

TOOLS AND MATERIALS

» *Corrugated cardboard box that's about 12" × 8" × 3" (30 × 20 × 8 cm) (a bit smaller than a shoebox)*
» *Masking tape*
» *Duct tape*
» *12" (30 cm) paint stirrers*
» *12 ml Luer Slip plastic syringes*
» *⅛" (3 mm) vinyl tubing*
» *Pipe cleaners*
» *Scissors*
» *Straws*
» *Scrap cardboard*
» *Plastic egg*
» *Self-stick googly eyes*
» *Index cards or card stock*
» *Pencil*
» *Bamboo skewers*

Material sources:

Plastic syringes and tubing are fantastic materials for making hydraulic and pneumatic-powered projects, but they're not available everywhere. If you ask nicely, your local pharmacy may give you a few syringes for free. Aquarium supply and hardware stores sell flexible plastic tubing. Make sure your syringe fits tightly in the tubing! Of course, as always, you can find these materials online.

1. Use four pieces of masking tape to strap down the longest flaps of the box.

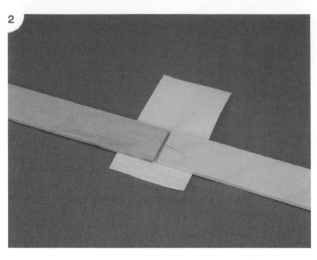

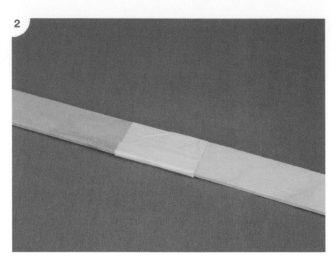

2. Create the pneumatic-powered hinge!

Start by placing the two paint stirrers end-to-end with a small gap between.
Cut a 3" (7.5 cm) piece of duct tape and lay it across both paint stirrers. Wrap the tape tightly.

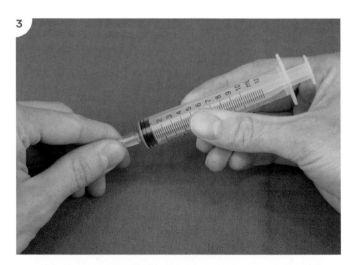

3. Fit the tubing onto the syringe nozzle.

Tip: Hold the tubing near the end to prevent it from bending as you push it onto the syringe.

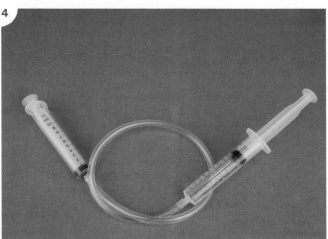

4. Fill a second syringe with 10 ml of air. Fit it onto the other end of the tubing. Try it out by alternately pushing the syringe plungers!

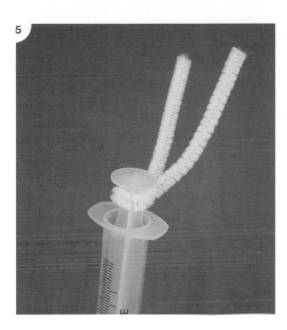

5. Tightly twist a pipe cleaner onto the end of the syringe plunger. If it slides around, apply a small piece of masking tape.

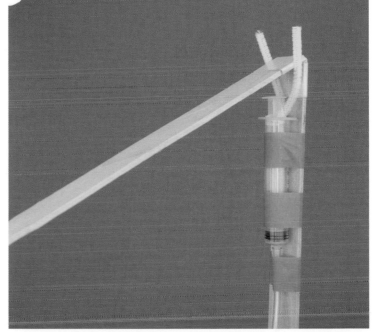

6. This step will determine how well your pneumatic hinge raises and lowers, so follow it carefully. First, completely empty the air out of the syringe with the pipe cleaner by pushing down the plunger. Use at least three pieces of tape to attach that syringe about 1" (2.5 cm) below the point where the two paint stirrers are connected.

<u>Important:</u> Make sure the twist in the pipe cleaner is right next to the upright paint stirrer, as shown in photo 6! If it's facing around, your lift won't go very high!

7. Tightly twist the pipe cleaner onto the paint stirrer. Tape it into place.

8. Test!

When you operate the syringe at the opposite end of the tubing, your pneumatic hinge should have a range of motion similar to that shown in these pictures.

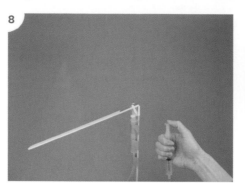

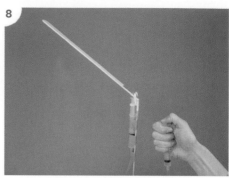

MINDSET: BE DETERMINED

9. Your pneumatic hinge may not work perfectly right away, and it might seem "good enough." However, innovation requires effort! Be determined to get your lift arm to meet the goal of a 12-inch (30 cm) range of motion, even if it requires some troubleshooting.

If the hinge doesn't rise:

- You might not have enough air in the pneumatic system. Make sure you have a total of 10 ml of air between both syringes.

- Make sure the twist in the pipe cleaner is positioned next to the paint stirrer.

- Try untaping the syringe and moving it closer to the spot where the paint stirrers are connected.

If the hinge doesn't lower:

- You might have too much air in the pneumatic system.

- Try untaping the syringe, and moving it farther from the spot where the paint stirrers are connected.

- The pipe cleaner attachment might be too loose. Try twisting it tighter around the syringe and around the paint stirrer.

10. Attach the paint stirrer with the syringe taped to it to the side of the box. Start with two horizontal pieces of tape.

11. Add two vertical pieces over the first ones. This will ensure that the paint stirrer doesn't tip over.

12. The pneumatic lift is done!

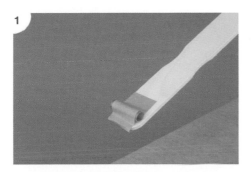

RAISE AND LOWER A LOAD!

1. <u>Here's a tip:</u> The platform that holds the load needs to stay level as the lift arm raises and lowers. To make that happen, add a pipe-cleaner hinge. Start by cutting a small piece of a straw and taping it to the tip of the lift arm.

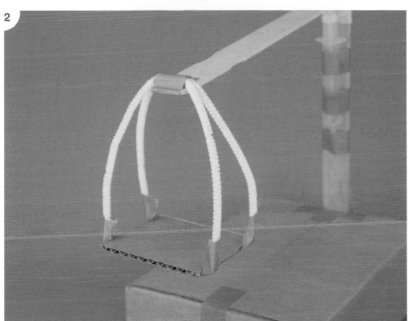

2. Fit two pipe cleaners through the straw and tape the ends to the corners of a small cardboard square. Try raising and lowering the lift. You'll notice that the platform stays level!

3. The next step is to select your load. In my example, the load will be a plastic egg with googly eyes because my pneumatic lift is going to be one of those machines that helps people reach high places, like a cherry picker.

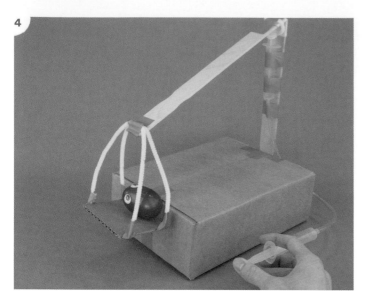

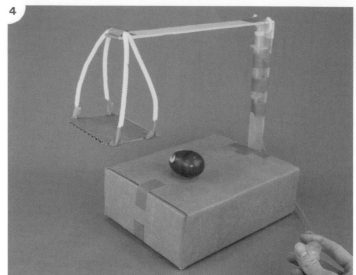

4. <u>Test:</u> **Place your load on the platform and lift it up!**
My initial test didn't work out so well!

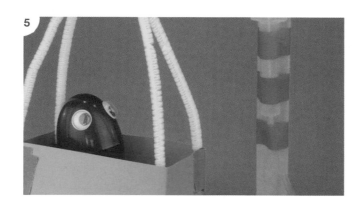

PROCESS: EVALUATE AND REDESIGN

5. Time to take a close look at your design and figure out a way to keep the load on the platform. What kinds of walls or restraints can you build? How can you keep the load in if the hinge raises or lowers very fast? Redesign your platform. Your design solution will depend on what kind of load you are carrying.

MINDSET: BE DETERMINED

6. Keep testing, evaluating, and redesigning until you can successfully raise your load to the highest point possible! If, after many redesigns, your load keeps falling out, try a totally different platform design. Giving up on an idea that doesn't work doesn't mean you've failed—it means you've learned at least one thing that doesn't work! Innovators look at setbacks as opportunities to learn.

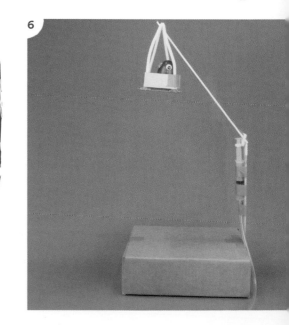

7. For added fun, transform your pneumatic lift into a vehicle! Start creating the wheels by tracing a cup onto scrap cardboard and cutting out the circles. The circles will be easier to cut out if they are on small pieces of cardboard.

7

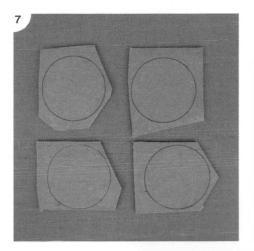

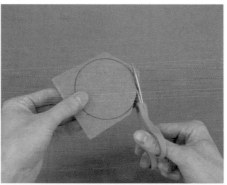

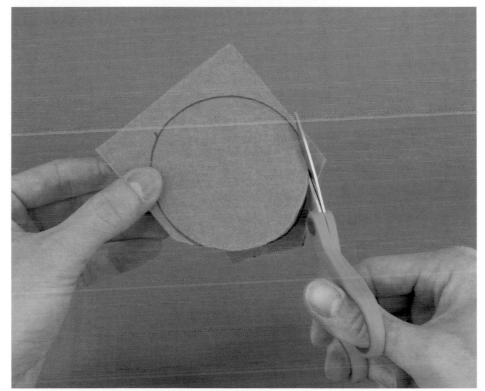

KNOWLEDGE: SKILLS AND TECHNIQUES

Cutting circles can be challenging, especially from cardboard. Here's a key technique: Keep the scissors in the same position and rotate the cardboard as you cut. This makes it much easier to cut circles because you can keep your wrist straight while cutting.

For added flair, decorate the wheels with colored tape or paint before cutting them out.

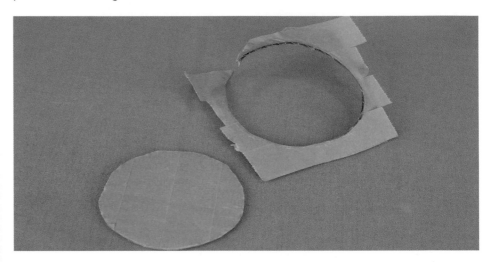

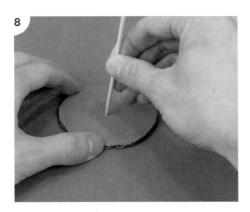

8. Use a bamboo skewer to pierce a hole in the middle of each wheel. Don't worry if it's not perfect; just do your best to center it.

9. Tape the skewers onto the bottom of the box, a few inches (5 cm) in from the ends. Use at least two pieces of tape, and make sure the skewers are parallel with the box's edge.

10. Fit the wheels onto the skewers, and give the box a push. (It'll work best on carpet.) You might notice that some of the wheels start to wobble or lean. In that case, use the side of the box to help keep the wheels upright in the next step!

11. Push the wheel against the cardboard box so it's upright, then slip a little scrap of cardboard onto the skewer. Make sure the scrap is pointing up and down, as shown.

12. Tightly pinch a piece of tape around the scrap and skewer. This will help push the wheel against the side of the box, which will create extra friction. The wheels won't turn as easily, but this will keep the wheels upright.

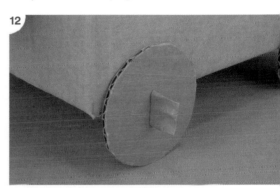

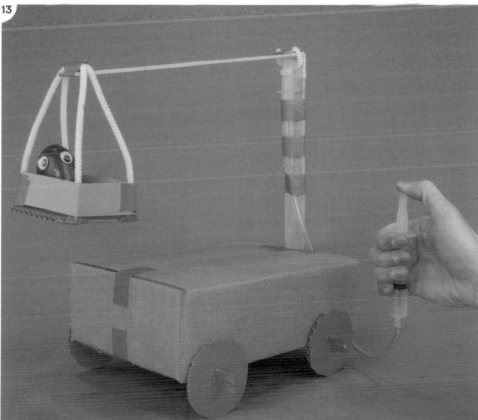

13. Complete! Or is it?
What else can you add to your pneumatic machine? What about a driver's seat? Or a ladder from the ground to the top of the box? Or maybe you can create a second pneumatic-powered hinge that performs another action!

DESIGN CHALLENGE

Build an automaton that

- Includes at least two moving characters
- Operates smoothly and reliably
- Has a cohesive theme

Bonus: Includes a pulley-powered element

CARDBOARD AUTOMATON

Inspired by an activity from the Exploratorium Museum in San Francisco, California, the cardboard automaton is built with common materials and techniques, yet offers a wide array of complex motions! When the crank is turned, the spaceship and UFO bob up and down and spin in circles!

TOOLS AND MATERIALS

- » *Corrugated cardboard box, at least 12" long, 10" high, and 8" deep (30 × 25 × 20 cm)*
- » *Masking tape*
- » *Scissors*
- » *Pencil*
- » *Ruler*
- » *Pencil sharpener*
- » *¼" (6 mm)-thick dowel that's about 4" (10 cm) longer than your box*
- » *Corks*
- » *Craft stick*
- » *Hot glue gun and glue*
- » *3 oz (88 ml) paper cups*
- » *Thin drinking straw*
- » *Bamboo skewers*
- » *Craft foam*
- » *⅛" × 7" (3 mm × 17.8 cm) rubber band (size #117b)*

Material substitutions

Corks: I use corks because they can be pierced with a skewer and they provide some weight, which helps the cam follower rest firmly on the cam. But you can use thick packaging foam or multiple layers of craft foam instead. If you need more weight, add a metal washer.

Tip: Find Free Corks
Restaurants are apt to have a lot of corks. If you ask politely, your server might give you a few!

1. Prepare the box.
Close up the flaps on one side of the box with masking tape. Use the scissors (and some muscle!) to cut off the four box flaps on the other side.

Tip: Use the right-sized box.
The rotating mechanism might bump the inside of the box if it's too small. Make sure your box is at least 8" (20 cm) deep.

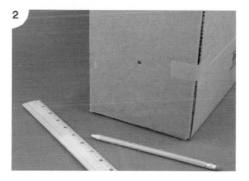

2. Find the center of each side of the box.
Draw lines from opposing corners to make an X. Use a sharpened pencil to poke a hole through the middle of the X. Repeat on the other side.

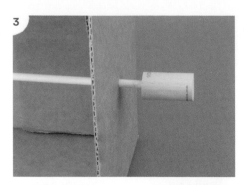

3. Install the crankshaft.
Cut the dowel to about 4" (10 cm) longer than the width of the box. Sharpen one end of the dowel and insert it through the holes in the box. Push a cork onto the sharpened end of the dowel.

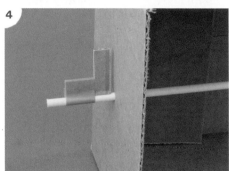

4. Cut out an L-shaped piece of cardboard and tape to the other end as shown. This will prevent the dowel from sliding into the box too far.

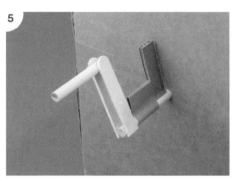

5. Make the crank handle.
Cut a 4" (10 cm) piece of dowel (or break off a piece of skewer). Snap the craft stick in half, and hot glue the two pieces of craft stick onto the end of the crankshaft with the small piece of dowel between, forming an L. Sandwiching the dowels between the craft sticks forms a very sturdy crank.

6. Create the cam-follower support.
Glue a small paper cup onto the top of the box where you want your first moving element to be. Use a sharpened pencil to pierce a hole through the cup and through the box.

KNOWLEDGE: CONCEPTS AND FACTS—CAMS AND CAM-FOLLOWERS

Cams are parts of machines that transform a circular spinning motion into a linear up-down or side-to-side motion. The shape, size, position, and number of the cams create different kinds of motion! Cam followers are the objects that are moved by the cam. Look at the drawings on page 87: The cam followers are the horizontal circles that rest on top of the cams.

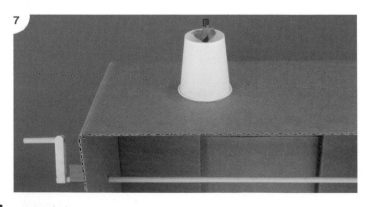

7. Cut a straw in half and insert it through the hole. Tape it in place to prevent it from sliding around. This helps reduce friction and ensures that the cam follower doesn't wobble.

MINDSET: BE VISIONARY

8. Your automaton does not yet exist and it's up to you to create a vision for it. What types of characters or objects will be in your scene and how will those things move?

Once you imagine a clear and unique vision for the automaton scene you want to create, you can go about making a design plan to bring your vision to life.

Since the shape and size of your cams affect how your automaton elements will move, your vision will need to include both mechanical and visual elements. Look closely at the photos and illustrations of different cams and try to visualize how each design will work.

Then pick a cam shape to try that you think will match the motion you envision.

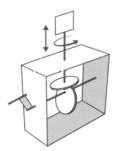
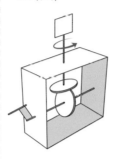

8

Round cam: level circular motion

Off-center oval cam: up-and-down, and circular motion

Shell-shaped cam: Slowly rise and quickly fall, and circular motion

Two off-center cams: quickly bob up and down, and turn side to side

9

10

9. Make your cams.
Different shapes produce different motions. Cut out a circle that's 3" to 4" (7.5 to 10 cm) in diameter. Pierce a hole into it. The position of the hole affects how much the cam follower will move up and down. The farther from the center, the greater the up-down movement.

Note:
There are many more cam-shape possibilities than I could fit into this book, so experiment with a few options before settling on one. Try off-center cams, snail-shaped cams, or even more than one cam with a single cam follower!

10. Prepare the cams for installation.
Cut a slit from the outside of the cam to the hole. Glue an L-shaped piece of cardboard about 1.5" × 1.5" (3.8 × 3.8 cm) onto the cam right next to the hole. This will be used to prevent the cam from wobbling.

11. Slip the cam onto the crankshaft through the slit.

12. Position the cam under the cam-follower support. Tape the cardboard L onto the crankshaft.

13. Make the cam follower
Cut a 3" to 4" (7.5 to 10 cm) circle and glue a cork to the center. Depending on the size of your box, you may need to cut the cork in half with a kitchen knife or by carefully working at it with scissors. Poke a hole into the cork with a skewer.

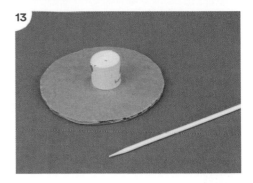

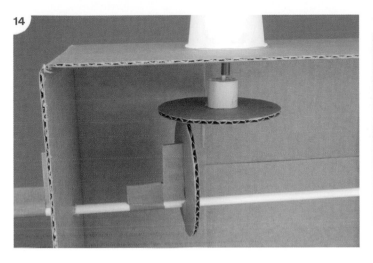

14. Install the cam-follower
Hold the cam follower above the cam and drop a skewer into the straw. Fit the skewer into the hole you made in the cork.

15. Test it out! Remember, your goal is to have motions that work smoothly and reliably.

PROCESS: EVALUATE AND REDESIGN

16. There are a lot of moving parts in this project and they may not move smoothly at first. Your cam might get stuck or the cam follower support might be crooked. Take the time to slowly rotate the crankshaft and look closely at your automaton to find out if, and why, your cams aren't working just right. You can easily reposition the cam by untaping it from the crankshaft and moving it. If you need to remake your cam, just slip it off and try again! If you're having trouble evaluating the quality of the motion, attach a small piece of tape to the top of the skewer and watch how the flag moves when you turn the crank.

17. Repeat steps 6 to 16 to create more motions with different cams.

CREATE THE SCENE

1. Add your characters!
My example features a space ship and a UFO. You can layer craft foam to create features that seem to pop, like rocket flames or UFO lights. Get creative with other decorative materials like pipe cleaners.

2. Create another moving element!
I decided to add a spinning star to complement my space scene. Here's how to do it with a rubber band pulley.

3. Create the rubber band pulley.
Glue a folded piece of cardboard around the back corner of the box on the side opposite the crank. Attaching the cardboard around a corner (to both the side and back of the box) creates a sturdy surface for the pulley.

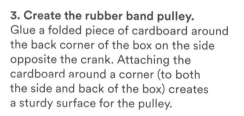

4

5

6

4. Glue a piece of cork and a 1" × 2" (2.5 × 5 cm) piece of cardboard onto the back side of the cardboard extension. The cork should be 9" (23 cm) from the crankshaft below.

5. Use a sharpened pencil to poke holes as shown. Install a 6" (15 cm) piece of dowel.

6. Temporarily remove one end of the short dowel to attach the 7" (17.8 cm) rubber band onto the crankshaft and the short dowel. Turn the crank. The short dowel should turn with the crankshaft. If the rubber band is too loose, reattach the cork-cardboard piece a little higher. If it's too tight, reattach it lower.

7. Attach your moving element to the end of the short dowel and continue embellishing. Add more elements that help tell the story. Get creative with your materials. Try finding things that jiggle and wiggle with cam-follower motion, like pipe cleaners or folded paper. Try covering the cardboard surfaces with colorful construction paper to bring more vibrancy to your scene. It's yours to customize!

7

REENTRY CAPSULE

When astronauts go into space, they need a safe way to return to Earth. One way to do this is with a reentry capsule, which allows the astronauts to re-enter Earth's atmosphere. The capsule is designed to fall from space into Earth's atmosphere and to land safely. The inside needs to be designed to keep astronauts safe during the bumpy reentry ride!

DESIGN CHALLENGE

Build a reentry capsule that keeps a plastic egg astronaut intact when launched from the highest level possible.

TOOLS AND MATERIALS

- » 16 oz (473 ml) paper cup with lid
- » Duct tape
- » ⅛" × 3.5" (3 mm × 9 cm) rubber bands (size 33)
- » ¼" (6 mm) dowel, 24" (61 cm) long
- » 4½" (11.5 cm) craft sticks
- » Marker
- » Ruler
- » Plastic egg
- » Small metal washers or coins
- » Googly eyes
- » Cushiony materials (straws, pom-poms, foam, paper towels)

Material Limits = Creative Solutions

The easiest solution to this challenge is to stuff the cup with soft, absorbent material, but remember: Astronauts need room to breathe and use their hands! Encourage creative solutions by giving out only limited materials. I recommend one paper towel, one 5" × 8" (13 × 20 cm) piece of foam, and six straws.

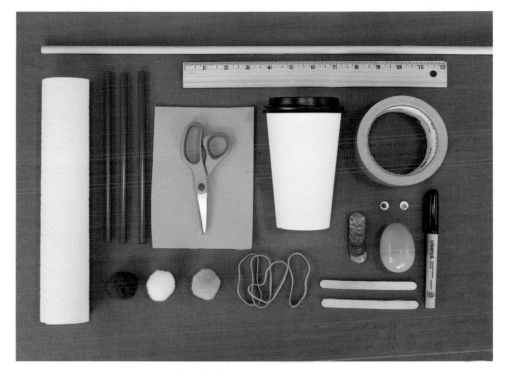

PREP

Create your astronauts

Place 10 coins or metal washers in the egg to give it some body weight. You might also give your egg some personality with googly eyes and a smile.

Create the capsule

An adult will need to prepare the capsule for younger kids.

Use a 1" × 4" (2.5 × 10 cm) piece of duct tape to attach two rubber bands to the side of a cup about 2" (5 cm) from the top. Apply two more pieces of tape across the first, as shown.

1. Create the launch stick. Use duct tape to attach two craft sticks to the end of the dowel so that only about ¼" (6 mm) is poking out at the end.

2. Loop the rubber bands onto the dowel as shown. Mark the spot on the dowel where the bottom of the cup touches. This is level 0.

3. Measure and mark 7 more levels that are about 1" (2.5 cm) apart. Write a number next to each to indicate the ever more challenging launch levels!

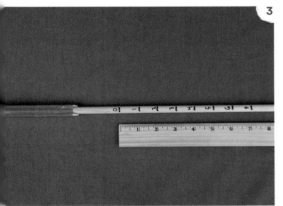

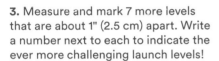

4. Time to cushion the capsule! Carefully arrange the cushiony material inside the capsule, and then place your astronaut inside and snap on the lid.

5. Countdown . . . 3 . . . 2 . . . 1 . . . launch!
Pull the capsule down to the level 1 mark, and release! When the capsule lands, open to see if the egg is intact, and then test again at the next higher level. I made it up to level 3 before . . . .

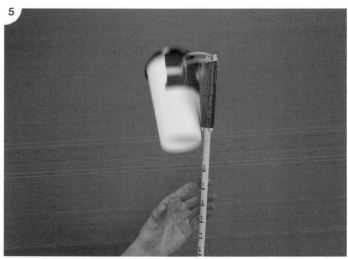

6. Oh no!
My astronaut broke open!
Time to redesign.

MINDSFT: BE COURAGEOUS

7. This won't be the last time the astronaut breaks open! Embrace the challenge of launching from the highest challenge level possible, even though you know it increases the risk of failure. When you step outside your comfort zone, you are bound to improve in unexpected ways—and so will your project!

PROCESS: REDESIGN

8. This time, I used all of my foam, and I cut up pieces of straw. I also loosely crumpled the paper towel to cover my astronaut's head!

9. Test again! After a few redesigns, I was able to safely launch and crash all the way to level 7!

CRASH TEST CAR

Making STEAM projects is super fun, but it's even more fun when the goal is to crash the thing you build! This crash-test car uses a rubber band slingshot to propel it at high speeds. Are you up for the challenge of keeping your driver safe? Then put on your reflective mindset goggles, buckle up, and begin!

DESIGN CHALLENGE

Build a car that

- Doesn't cover the crash-test buddy's eyes
- Keeps the crash-test buddy safely inside the car without taping it in
- Prevents the crash-test buddy's head from touching the ground if the car flips over

TOOLS AND MATERIALS

- » *Masking tape*
- » *A new #2 pencil*
- » *5" × 8" (13 × 20 cm) piece of corrugated cardboard*
- » *Drinking straws*
- » *Scissors*
- » *Wood turnings or plastic wheels*
- » *6" to 7" (15 to 18 cm) dowel or bamboo skewer that fits your wheels*
- » *⅛" × 3.5" (3 mm × 8.9 cm) rubber band size #33*
- » *Plastic egg*
- » *Small coins or metal washers*
- » *Googly eyes (optional)*
- » *Permanent marker (optional)*
- » *Card stock or index cards*
- » *Pipe cleaners*
- » *Scrap of cardboard*

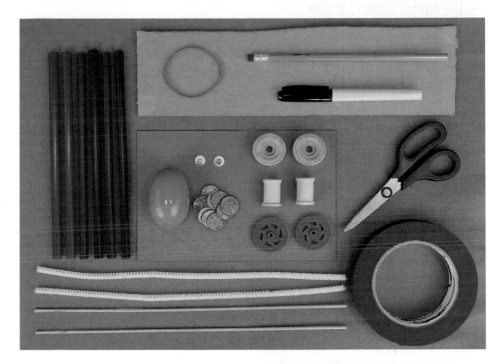

WHAT ABOUT THE WHEELS?

A little-known secret in the world of STEAM projects is that there is no good DIY solution for project wheels. I strongly recommend buying specialty materials, such as wooden spools, for the car wheels, or purchasing plastic wheels that are created for these kinds of projects. It'll make a big difference in how well your project works! Whatever your choice, also purchase dowels or skewers that fit your wheels.

PREP

Set up the launcher
Find a long, smooth section of floor. Use overlapping pieces of tape to secure a brand new pencil to the floor as shown. Be sure the eraser is pointing in the direction you intend the car to travel.

Cut the cardboard
For young kids, you'll need to cut cardboard into 5" × 8" (13 × 20 cm) pieces.

1. Make the wheels.
Tape a drinking straw to each of the short ends of the cardboard. Trim off the excess so that the straws only poke out a tiny bit past the edges of the cardboard. Make sure the straws are lined up straight with the edges of the cardboard.

2. Insert the dowels through the straws.
Fit the wheels onto the ends of the dowels.

3. If your wheels are loose on the dowels and slide off, wrap a narrow piece of tape around the ends of the dowels.

4. Decide which end of the car will be the front, and attach a rubber band to it using at least two layers of tape so it doesn't pull off easily.

KNOWLEDGE: CONCEPTS AND FACTS

There's a word called *crashworthiness*. It refers to how safe something is when it crashes. Did you know that scientists and engineers purposely crash real cars to test how safe they are? It's true! They place human-size dolls full of special sensors inside the car. The sensors tell the scientists what might happen if a real person were in a crash. For this project, you'll create a crash-test buddy to help you evaluate the crashworthiness of your car.

5. Make your crash-test buddy.
Place ten coins or small washers inside the plastic egg to give it a little body weight. Snap the egg shut, and provide your buddy with a personality. I personally like to add googly eyes and a goofy smile.

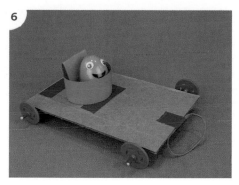

6. Every car needs a safe seat. Fold a strip of paper into a W shape. Bend the two ends down and tape them flat against the cardboard as shown. Use more paper to improve the seat so it can hold your crash test buddy.

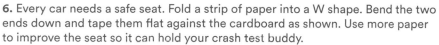

7. You want to make sure your buddy doesn't fly out and get hurt when the car crashes, so you'll need to make a seatbelt. The challenge is to make a seatbelt that holds the buddy in but doesn't cover it up completely. Your crash-test buddy needs to see! And remember: you can't tape your buddy in place! How would that feel, getting in and out of the car? Ouch!

8. It's test time!
Do a trial run straight across the floor and into a wall to see how your car moves and how your buddy does inside. Place the car over the pencil with the wheels on either side. Loop the rubber band over the tip of the eraser. Pinch the very back of the car. Pull back on the rubber band as far as you can—and release!

Take a moment to evaluate your test: Did your crash-test buddy stay in the seat? If not, how did it fall out? What can you do to redesign the seat so your buddy stays in next time?

MINDSET: BE COURAGEOUS

9. When you spend time and energy to build something, it can take courage to put your design at risk by crashing it! You might be worried about breaking your project, but innovators know that some of the best lessons can be learned by stretching yourself to try new things. If something breaks, you'll find a way to fix it and you'll learn something by doing so!

PROCESS: TEST, EVALUATE, AND REDESIGN

10. Time to level up the testing with a new challenge! Innovators are always looking for ways to improve their projects, even if they're already working. Try harder and harder challenges to discover ways you might redesign your car to make it better. Every time your design fails a crash test, it's an opportunity to discover a weak point in your design and make improvements.

After this next challenge, you can try testing with taller ramps, a more powerful launcher, or adding additional passengers!

11. Second challenge
Prevent the crash-buddy's head from touching the ground when the car flips over! For this, we'll need to build a car frame.

Create and test your own unique car frame design, using the taping techniques from the Straw Tower project (page 38).

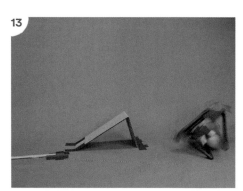

12. Set up the rollover crash test.
Create a ramp by cutting a scrap of cardboard to about 12" (30 cm) long and at least 4" (10 cm) wide. Make a 3" to 4" (7.5 to 10 cm) bend in the cardboard at one end. This will be the ramp. Position it so that only one set of the car's wheels will go up the ramp. Tape the ends securely to the floor as shown.

13. Launch the car just like before.
This time it will flip over!

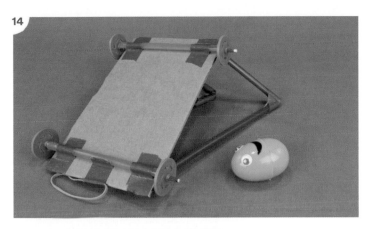

14. Oh no! My buddy fell out and my car frame is bent. Time to evaluate and redesign again. When your design fails, ask yourself what went wrong and then focus on finding a solution to those problems. I probably need to work on my seatbelt design and strengthen the frame. What redesign ideas do you get from your crash test failure?

16. Once your car is safe, you can start embellishing it. One idea is to add paper walls. In this example, I cut out triangles to fit the sides of my car. I also made windows by poking holes in the paper, then using scissors to cut out the inside shapes.

15. I've redesigned my car seat and frame. I won't share too much about what I did because the goal is to test and evaluate your own unique ideas. Keep testing and redesigning until you have a car that keeps your crash-test buddy safe every time.

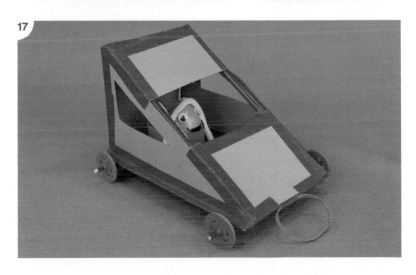

17. Use long pieces of tape when attaching the paper to give your car a snappy-looking outline.

What else can you do to personalize your super safe car? Add a steering wheel? An exhaust pipe? A vanity license plate? Go for it!

DESIGN CHALLENGE

Build a spinning ride that
- Spins fast
- Safely seats at least two riders without covering their faces or taping them in place

SPINNING RIDE

You've probably seen a spinning amusement park ride, like a Ferris wheel, scrambler ride, or a carousel. When scientists and engineers design those rides, the safety of the riders is the number one priority. Now it's your turn to create your own visionary, high-speed spinning ride, and your goal is to make it super fun but also super safe for the riders!

TICKETS
$1.00

TOOLS AND MATERIALS

- » 9" × 6" × 4" (23 × 15 × 10 cm) or similarly sized corrugated box
- » Scrap piece of cardboard
- » Masking tape
- » Hot glue gun and glue sticks
- » Sharpened pencil
- » Scissors
- » ¼" (6 mm) dowel, 6" (15 cm) long
- » Cotton string
- » Plastic straws
- » Cardboard cake circles
- » Ruler or yardstick
- » Index cards
- » Plastic eggs
- » Googly eyes
- » Colorful markers
- » Pipe cleaners

Material Substitutions

Cardboard cake circles: Many craft stores and some grocery stores sell cake circles, but you can substitute by tracing a dinner plate onto a scrap piece of cardboard and cutting out the circle with scissors.

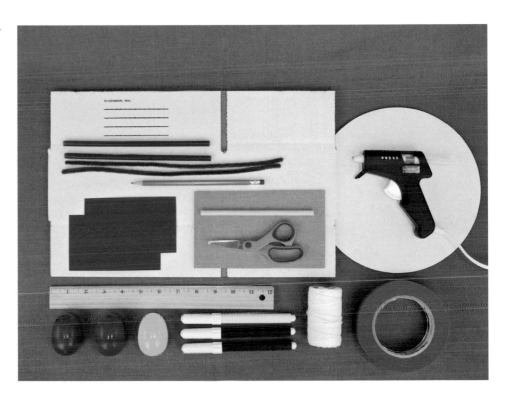

1. Start the spinning ride base.
Tape one side of the box closed. Cut a small scrap of cardboard about 2" × 3" (5 × 7.5 cm) and tape it into a closed loop or triangle. Hot glue the cardboard loop onto the bottom of the box near the middle, but not in the exact center. This will support the spinning dowel. When you're done, tape the box closed.

2. Make an access hatch!
Use a sharp pencil to poke four holes into the side of the box, and then use scissors to cut a rectangular door. Leave one side of the rectangle uncut for the hinged door. Poke a hole in the top of the box above the cardboard loop and insert the dowel.

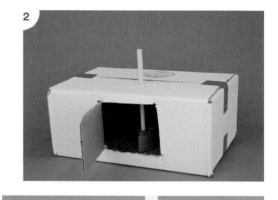

3. Cut a piece of cotton string about 16" (40.5 cm) long. Lay the string on some scrap cardboard or paper and carefully apply hot glue to one end. Wait for it to cool a little bit so the glue is just tacky. Pick it up, being careful not to accidentally touch the glue!

4. Carefully touch the glued string to the dowel inside the box, so that it sticks. Give the dowel a few turns, and the string will wind around it! When the glue has cooled, pinch a piece of masking tape onto the spot where the string and dowel join to give it some extra strength.

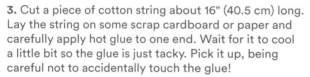

5. Use the pencil point to poke a hole in the side of the box and pull the string through it. Cut a short piece of straw and tape it to the end of the string to make a handle.

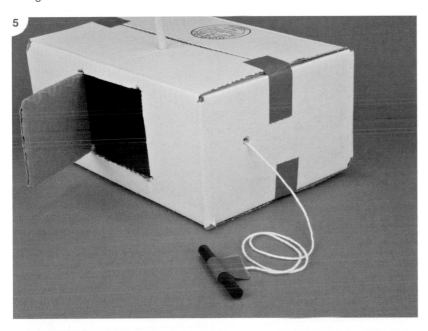

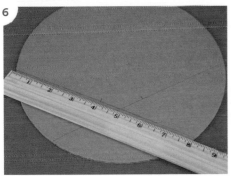

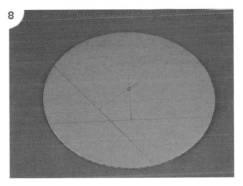

6. Time to build the spinning platform. The ride spins the fastest when the exact center of the platform is attached to the dowel, so we're going to use a little geometry trick to find the very middle! Use a ruler to draw two lines (chords) across the circle from edge to edge. In this case, both of my lines are 8" (20 cm). Find the center of each line, and mark the spot.

7. Place the long side of an index card on one of the lines on the circle with the corner of the index card on the center mark. Trace along the short side of the index card. Repeat with the other line.

8. The intersection of those lines is the exact center of the circle—pretty neat!

9. Ready to mount the platform! Cut two small strips of cardboard, and hot glue half of each one onto the dowel. Wrap tape around the glued ends of both, and then spread the other halves apart, level with the end of the dowel.

10. Apply hot glue onto the cardboard scraps and, while looking at the underside of the cardboard circle, center the circle on the dowel. When the glue has completely dried, wind the string around the dowel, and pull on the handle to give it a test!

MINDSET: BE VISIONARY

11. Make safe and secure seats for your riders.
There are many ways to solve the challenge without taping your riders in place or covering their faces. Think about all the different ways you can create sides, walls, or straps. How can you bend, fold, or combine materials to meet your unique vision? It's up to you to find a way that works best for your ride. Imagine creative solutions to keep your riders safe! Be open to trying ideas that don't look like normal seats, and think of ways to use materials in unusual ways.

PROCESS: TEST, EVALUATE, AND REDESIGN

12. Once you've built two seats, it's time to test! Start spinning the ride slowly, and then increase the speed. If one of the riders flies out, stop! Evaluate what happened: Why do you think the rider fell out? What could you redesign to keep your rider in? Make adjustments, test again, and keep going until both riders stay safely inside, even when spinning very fast!

KNOWLEDGE: CONCEPTS AND FACTS

Centrifugal force pushes spinning things away from the center of rotation. In this project, when they spin, the riders are pushed away from the center of the circle, which can cause them to fly out of their seats. As you redesign, think about what you can do to prevent your egg-riders from being flung outwards, over the edge of the ride.

Tip: Be sure that the seats are exactly opposite each other, and build them identically. The more uneven the weight, the more the ride will wobble and slow down!

13. The next step is to make your ride eye-catching! One way to do this is with alternating color patterns. These colors will blend together when they spin and create an optical illusion!

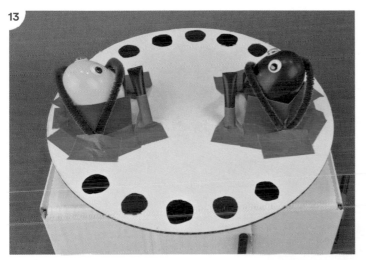

14. When the ride spins, the eye sees both colors in the same place at once. In this example, the blue and red blend together to make purple! The key is to color areas that will appear to overlap when spun. In this example, I colored only the outer edge of the circle to ensure the colors blur. Experiment with different color combinations to create some cool optical illusions!

15. The ride doesn't have to stop here! Keep decorating and adding other fun features, like a ticket booth, or maybe a name for your ride, or add another two seats!

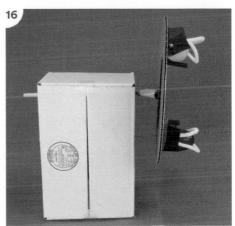

16. Consider making a completely different ride, like a Ferris wheel! You can create this type of ride by putting the dowel through both sides of the box (you won't need the cardboard loop from step 1). Everything else is the same—just turned on its side!

6

BIOMECHANICS

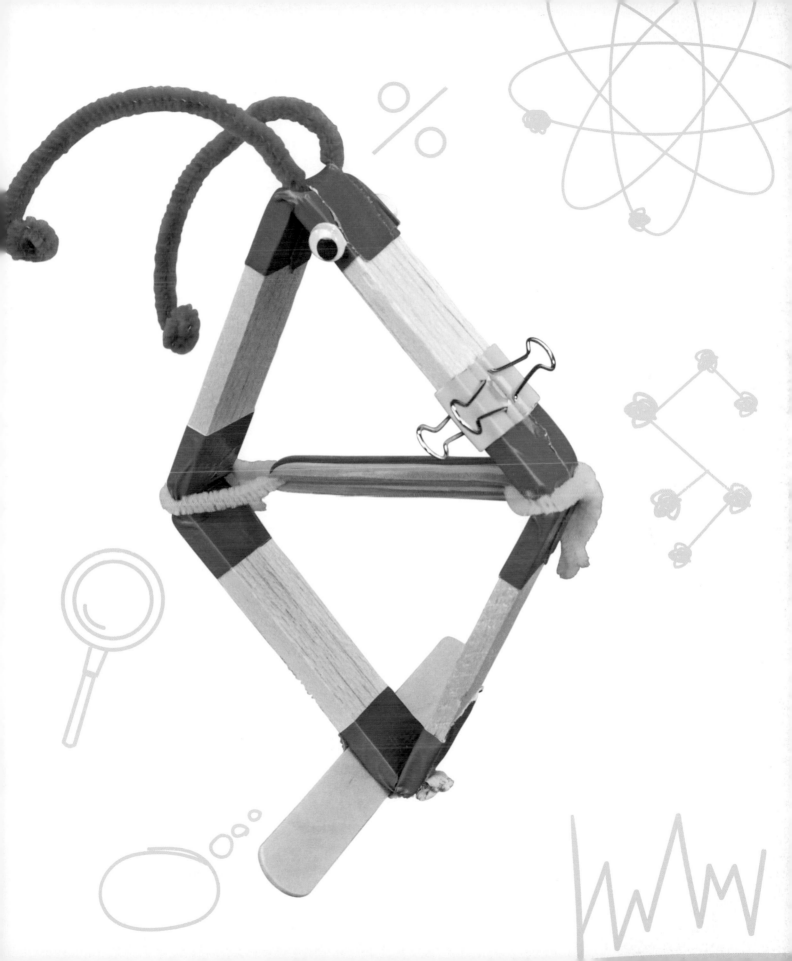

HUNGRY OCTOPUS

Did you know that the octopus is a predator? That means it hunts for smaller sea animals to eat! It does this by using its tentacles to snatch and pull prey into its mouth. This project mimics octopus tentacles with pipe cleaners. Pull on the pipe cleaners and your octopus gets to grab and eat its favorite food: Ping-Pong balls!

DESIGN CHALLENGE

Build an octopus that
- Has eight tentacles
- Can pick up a Ping-Pong ball

TOOLS AND MATERIALS

» *8 oz (236 ml) paper cup*
» *Sharpened pencil*
» *Scissors*
» *Craft foam*
» *6" (15 cm) craft stick*
» *Masking tape*
» *Pipe cleaners*
» *Ping-Pong ball*
» *Self-stick googly eyes*

Material substitutions

Ping Pong ball: You can use any small, lightweight object like a plastic egg, vending-machine toy capsule, Wiffle ball, or even a tightly balled up piece of copy paper.

Don't substitute paper for craft foam. The foam is much more flexible and durable, which is important for this project.

PREP (OPTIONAL)

Cut the foam strips
For especially young kids, you might need to cut the foam into ¾" × 6" (2 × 15 cm) strips. The size doesn't need to be precise. Use a paper cutter to speed up the prep.

1. Carefully poke a hole in the bottom of a paper cup with a sharpened pencil.

2. Insert closed scissors through the hole, and give it a twist to make the hole bigger. This will make it easier to put all the pipe cleaners through.

PROCESS: CREATE

You'll be making up to eight tentacles, so it's time to start creating each one!

3. Begin by cutting out a strip of foam.
You can use a 6" (15 cm) craft stick as a size guide: The foam strips and the stick should be about the same length and width. If the foam strips are too wide, you won't have enough room to fit all eight!

4. Tape the end of the foam strip right next to the opening of the cup.

5. Put a pipe cleaner through the hole in the cup. Tape the end of the pipe cleaner to the end of the foam.

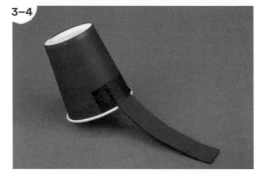

6. Repeat with another foam strip on the opposite side. Give it a test: Pull on the pipe cleaners to make the tentacles pinch inward. My octopus doesn't have enough tentacles to pick up the Ping-Pong ball yet, so I need to add more!

MINDSET: BE DETERMINED

7. The tentacles will work best if they can work together. Put in the effort to create all eight tentacles the same way. Do your best to make each one the same size and shape and tape them carefully. If you get tired of building partway through, take a minute to play with your "quadruped" or "hexapod" and revel in your progress before moving on. Sometimes to persevere, it helps to celebrate mini-accomplishments along the way toward reaching your big goal.

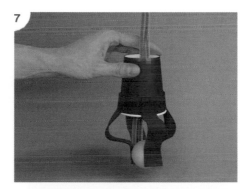

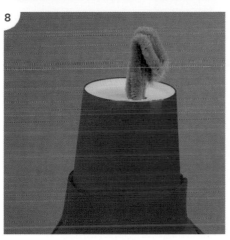

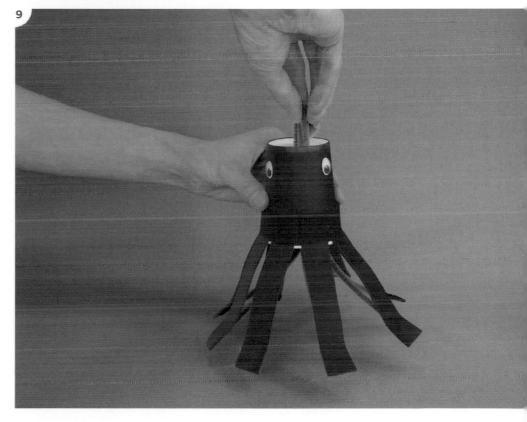

8. Keep going and create a total of eight tentacles!
When you're done, line up the ends of all the pipe cleaners and bend them. This will help to make sure the tentacles extend and retract evenly.

9. Give your octopus some personality by adding googly eyes, then take a look around: What else can you pick up with your hungry octopus? Hmm . . . that garlic clove looks like lunch!

GRASSHOPPER

Did you know that grasshoppers have a spring-like mechanism in their knees? Their legs are like little catapults. They store potential elastic energy in their legs, and then release it all at once when they jump, just like a rubber band.

In fact, you can use rubber bands to build your own high-jumping grasshopper. With some testing, redesigning, and reflection, yours could jump as much as 4 feet (1.2 m) into the air!

DESIGN CHALLENGE

Build a grasshopper that
- Can jump at least 24" (61 cm) upwards
- Can jump at least 12" (30.5 cm) sideways

TOOLS AND MATERIALS

- » ¼" × 1" (6 mm × 2.5 cm) piece of balsa wood
- » Ruler
- » Scissors
- » Duct tape
- » 6" (15 cm) jumbo craft stick or similar
- » Pipe cleaners
- » Rubber bands of assorted lengths and thicknesses
- » ½" (1.25 cm) binder clips
- » Foam mounting squares and googly eyes (optional)

Material Substitutions

Balsa wood: Balsa is easier to cut, but you can also use paint stirrers.

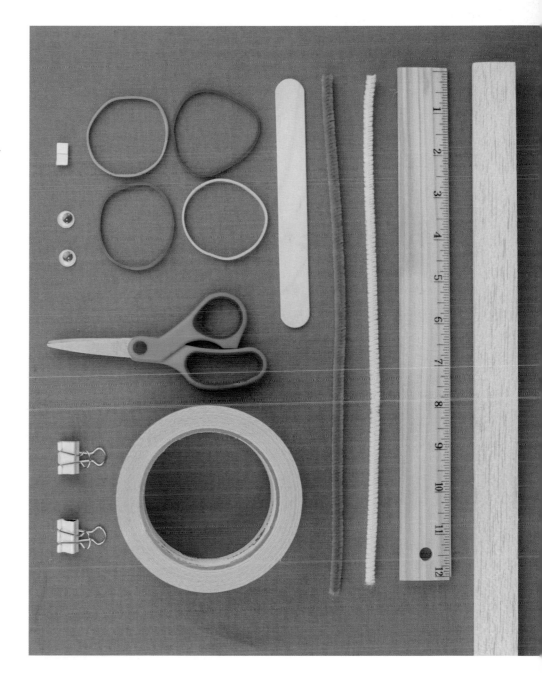

PREP

Cut the balsa

An adult is needed for this step. Balsa wood can be cut with scissors, but that can be tough for young kids. Cut four pieces of 4" (10 cm) balsa per grasshopper. If you use paint stirrers, prep the cut line by indenting it with a wire cutter. Then line up the indent with the edge of a table and snap it for a clean break.

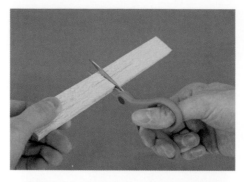

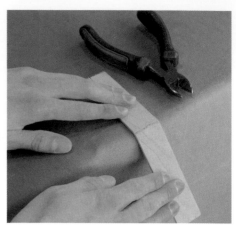

Cut the duct tape

In step 1, below, there's a technique that will help kids cut their own duct tape, but there's a learning curve that can be tricky to master. You might choose to pre-rip 3" (7.5 cm) pieces of tape.

1

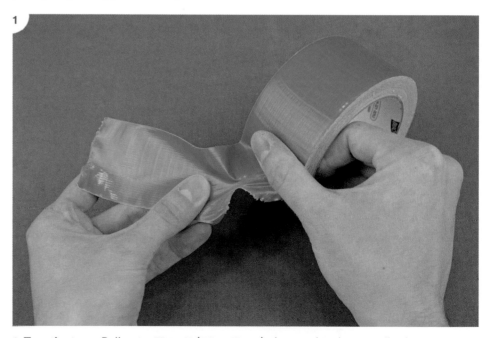

1. Tear the tape. Pull out a 3" to 4" (7.5 to 10 cm) piece and make a small snip in the edge with scissors. Grab hold on either side of the snip, and tear it the rest of the way.

2. Place the tape on the table, sticky-side-up. Lay two pieces of wood on top as shown. Be sure to leave a small gap between the pieces of wood. Tightly wrap the tape.

3. Repeat until all four pieces of wood are taped together in a line.

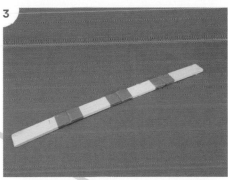

4. Here's where you'll need your buddy. Slowly fold the ends of the wood together until they're touching. One person will hold the wooden pieces end to end while the other person tapes it together, just as in step 2. The flexible square is done!

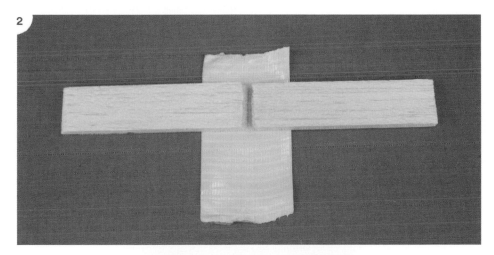

5. Tape a 6" (15 cm) craft stick onto one of the pieces of wood near a corner. This is the grasshopper's foot, which will help prevent it from tipping over.

6. Time to energize your grasshopper!
Stand it on its foot. Cut a pipe cleaner in half. Insert one of the pieces through a rubber band, then twist the pipe cleaner around one of the grasshopper's side joints. Twist it tightly so the pipe cleaner gets wedged into the gap between the wood pieces. Stretch the rubber band across the interior of the square and join it to the opposite joint with the other piece of pipe cleaner.

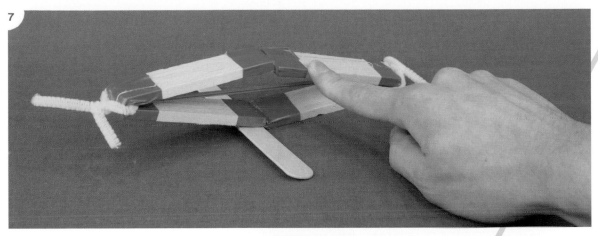

7. Get jumping! Press your grasshopper flat with one finger, and then let your finger slip off. Keep your hand clear of the grasshopper foot. Your grasshopper should leap into the air!

8. Try changing the number of rubber bands. Simply untwist the pipe cleaners, add another rubber band, and twist it back it back into place.

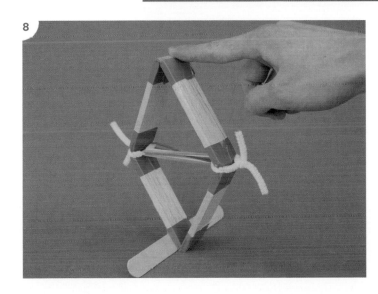

PROCESS:
TEST AND EVALUATE

9. If one rubber band is good, more must be better! Right? It's up to you to test different numbers and types of rubber bands to find out what works best. Guess how many rubber bands you think is best, then check by testing! Maybe more is better, but how many can you add until it becomes too hard to push the grasshopper all the way down?

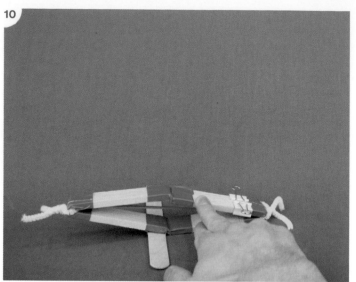

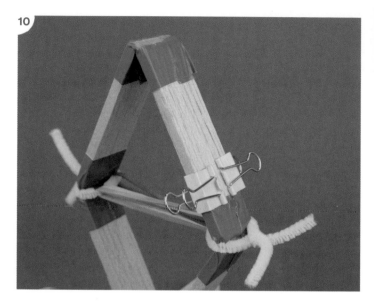

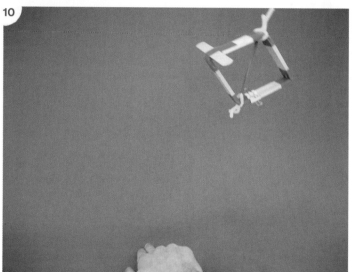

10. Grasshoppers can do more than just jump straight up—they can leap sideways, too!

Adding a little weight by attaching two small binder clips to one side will make your grasshopper leap to that side!

MINDSET: BE REFLECTIVE

11. To achieve the desired leap distances up and sideways, you could just make changes randomly—but that might not be very productive. Innovators always take time to think about what is and isn't working with their design and then make thoughtful, deliberate changes to improve their work.

Notice what is and isn't working in your design and then focus on how to fix something that isn't working without breaking something that is.

You may not always make choices that lead to better designs, but you will improve your ability to be reflective.

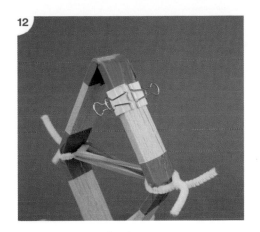

12

KNOWLEDGE:
CONCEPTS AND FACTS—CENTER OF MASS AND INERTIA

What made the grasshopper jump sideways? Before the binder clips were added, the grasshopper's center of mass was somewhere in the middle, so it jumped straight up. Now, one side is heavier than the other. The heavier side has more inertia—that means it takes more energy to get it moving. Placing the binder clips there also moves the center of mass away from the middle. So when the grasshopper jumps, the heavier side doesn't move as much as the other side. This means the whole grasshopper will rotate around the new center of mass, causing it to leap to the side!

PROCESS:
TEST AND EVALUATE

12. Try moving the binder clips to different parts the grasshopper to make your grasshopper jump in different ways! Start by guessing what position works best, then check by testing. With each test, take note of the position of the binder clips, and ask yourself, "How did that change the way it jumped?" Keep testing until you have the best sideways jump possible.

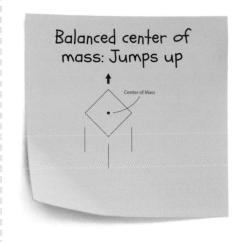

Balanced center of mass: Jumps up

Center of Mass

Offset center of mass: Jumps sideways

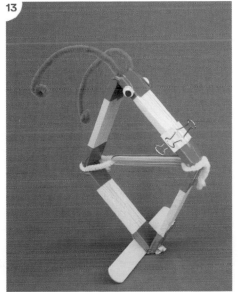

13

13. Optional: Make your grasshopper look more like, well, a grasshopper! Stick on a pair of googly eyes, and tape on some green antennae. Curl the antennae backward to give it an unmistakably grasshopper-y look!

LUNG LiFT

Did you know that your lungs are incredibly powerful? Try lying on your back and putting something heavy on your chest, like a thick book. When you breathe in and out, you'll see that your lungs can lift what's on your chest! The lungs are made of soft tissue, but they are protected by strong bones—ribs—that expand with them when we breathe. In this project, you'll re-create the power of the lungs with a plastic bag and protect it with a surface that can expand with it, creating a contraption that's powerful enough to lift heavy furniture!

DESIGN CHALLENGE

Build a lung lift that
– Doesn't bend
– Can lift a chair

TOOLS AND MATERIALS

» *Sealable plastic bag*
» *Scissors*
» *Straw*
» *Duct tape*
» *Corrugated cardboard*
» *6" (15 cm) jumbo craft sticks*
» *Masking tape*

Materials Limits: Creative Constraints

Limit the number of craft sticks that can be used to 8. If you are allowed to use an unlimited number of sticks, then the design challenge is too easy. Instead, focus on creating a resourceful arrangement of a small number of materials and rearranging them if necessary.

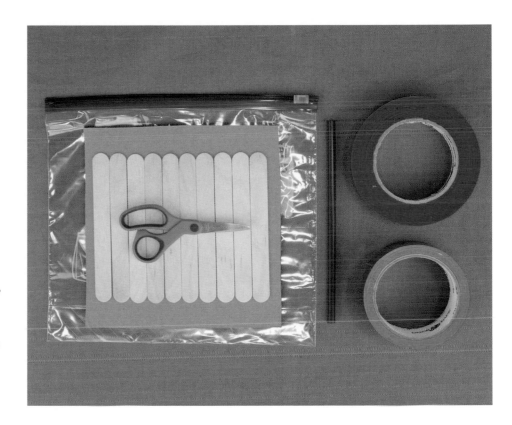

1. Let's get started!
Seal the top of the bag. Cut a very tiny piece off the corner of the plastic bag and insert a straw.

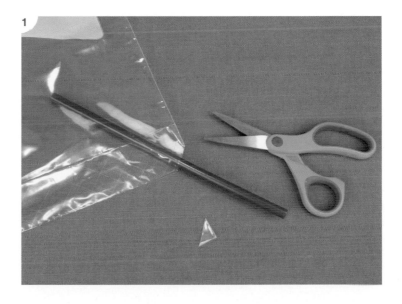

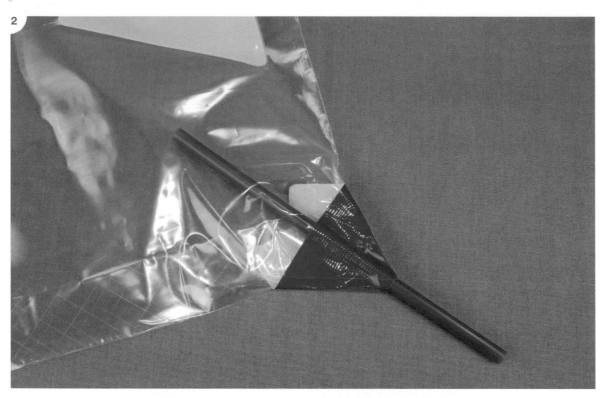

2. Fold a piece of tape around the straw and bag and press it together tightly to ensure an airtight seal. This works best if the sticky sides of the tape are pressed together.

3. Blow into the straw to inflate the bag and check for any air leaks before moving on. If you hear air escaping anywhere but the straw, apply another piece of tape.

4. Make a loop of duct tape, stick it to the middle of the cardboard, and then stick the cardboard onto the bag. The cardboard will prevent the bag from being punctured.

5. If you test it now, you'll find that the cardboard bends a lot, even if you try to lift a lightweight chair with it!

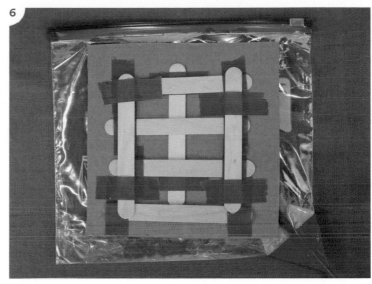

6. Tape up to eight of the craft sticks onto the cardboard to make it stronger. Since this is your design challenge, I'm not going to say much about why I arranged the sticks the way I did—it's up to you to find a design that keeps the cardboard sturdy.

PROCESS: TEST, EVALUATE, AND REDESIGN

7. Give it a test!
Inflate the lung lift to raise up a piece of furniture and notice how strong the cardboard pad is or isn't. Is it bending or breaking? If so, where can you add more materials to make the pad stronger? Make a change and test it again.

If you're able to successfully lift a light piece of furniture, try something heavier! Evaluate and redesign after each test to improve your lung lift's capacity. You'll be surprised at just how strong your lungs are.

MINDSET: BE COLLABORATIVE

8. One way to be collaborative is to use your strengths to support the work of others. In this project, someone else can support your work by giving you a broader perspective on how your project is working and by promoting safety.

It might be tricky to see what's going on when your head is so close to the floor and to your lung lift. Be collaborative by asking a friend to watch your lung lift as you test. Ask, "What part of the cardboard bent? How can I redesign to stop it from bending there?" Your friend had a better view than you, so listen to his or her perspective.

Secondly, as your project meets its goals, you'll be lifting heavier and heavier furniture ... right near your head! When testing, always have someone nearby on furniture-catching duty. If a chair or table leans too much, that person can catch it—you don't want heavy furniture falling on anyone or anything!

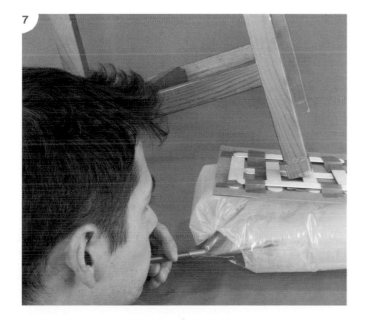

MECHANICAL HAND

Dedicated scientists and engineers have developed amazing technologies for creating artificial hands, feet, and limbs. This mechanical hand is decidedly low-tech but still cleverly engineered with articulated fingers that can bend, grasp, and pick things up. This is a challenging project, so get ready to be determined and persevere until the hand is working just right!

DESIGN CHALLENGE

Build a mechanical hand that

- Has at least three fingers

- Articulates smoothly

- Can pick up a sponge and a cup

- Can complete basic everyday tasks

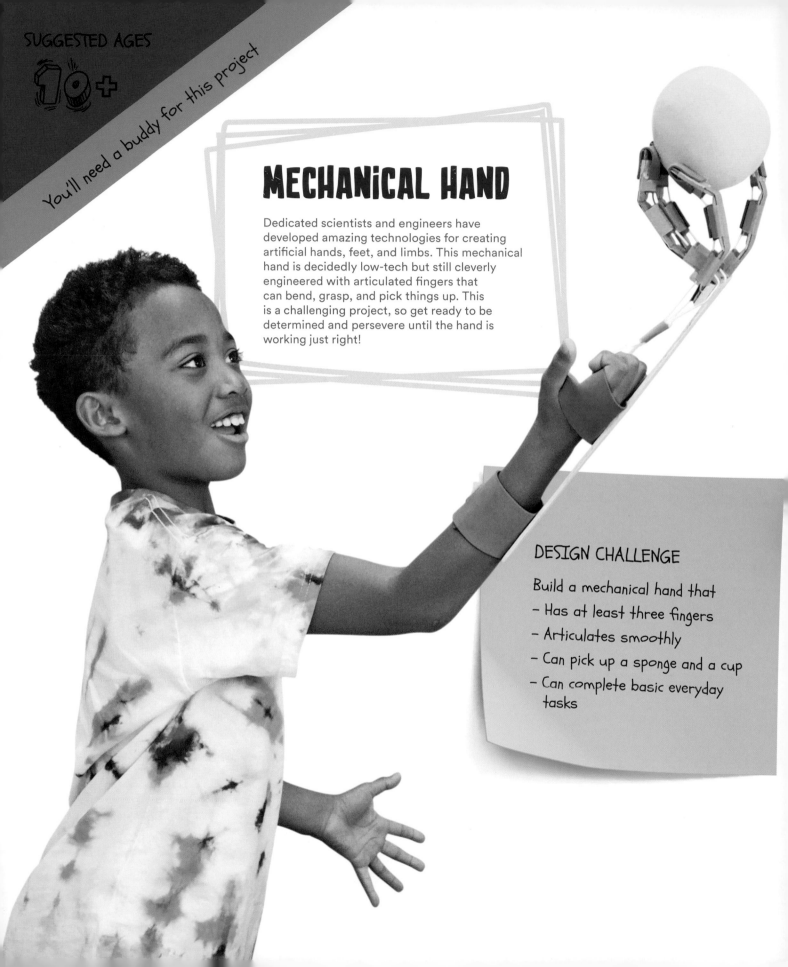

TOOLS AND MATERIALS

- » *Synthetic cork*
- » *Utility knife*
- » *Corrugated cardboard*
- » *Large scissors*
- » *Plastic straws*
- » *Masking tape*
- » *String*
- » *Paint stirrer*
- » *6" (15 cm) jumbo craft stick*
- » *Hot glue gun and glue stick*
- » *A few everyday objects (like a sponge and a cup)*
- » *Craft foam*

Material Substitutions

Corks: Corks provide a sturdy, upright surface for different appendages, and restaurants may give them to you for free if you ask nicely. Otherwise, you can substitute square wooden beads, ½" (13 mm) sections of square dowels, or similarly shaped materials.

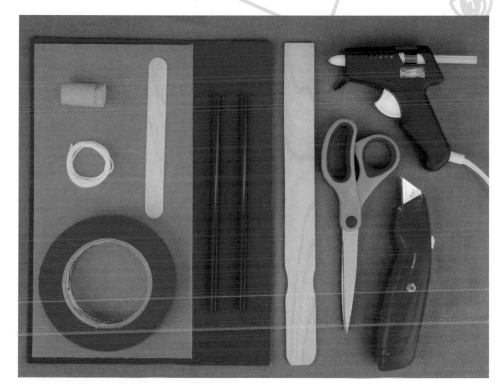

PREP

Cut the corks
An adult will need to use the utility knife to cut corks into quarters, as shown.

KNOWLEDGE: CONCEPTS AND FACTS

Did you know your fingers don't have muscles in them? The muscles that control your fingers are in your forearm! So what connects the muscles to your fingers? The answer is tendons—think of them as cables. The tendons are held in place inside your arm by ligaments—think of them as connectors. Annular ligaments (annular means "ring") are shaped like rings. Tendons slide through the rings, which keep them lined up where they should be. In this project, we'll use strings for our tendons and pieces of plastic straws as our annular ligaments.

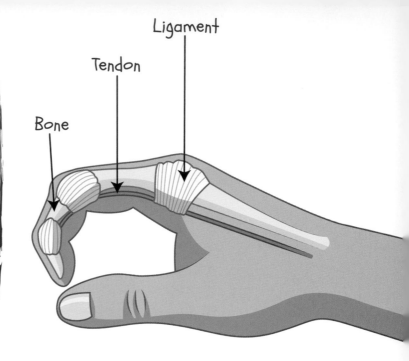

Bone · Tendon · Ligament

1. Start by making the fingers from strips of cardboard. Decide on the width of the fingers, and then bend the cardboard to that measurement. I made my fingers about ¾" (2 cm) wide and 6" (15 cm) long.

Tip: Make sure that the corrugations are going lengthwise along (rather than across) the fingers, as shown. This will greatly increase their strength.

2. Bending the cardboard before cutting will help you avoid accidental creases. If the cardboard gets creased, it will weaken. Use large scissors to cut the strips.

3. Create at least three fingers. I decided to make four. You can choose the shape and length of your fingers. Longer fingers can grab larger objects, but they may require more joints to work well. Shorter fingers will be more durable, but won't be able to grab large items.

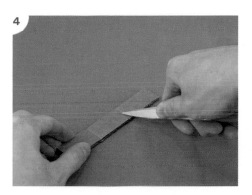

4

4

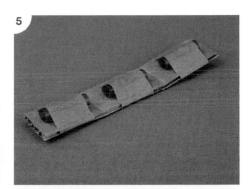

5

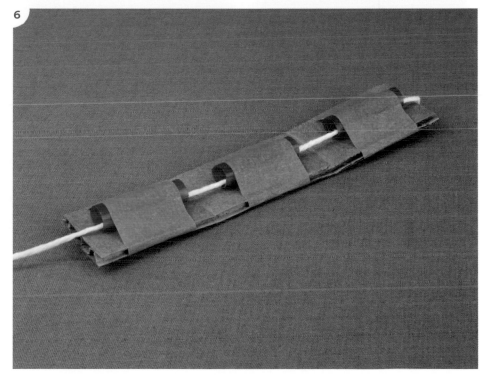

6

4. Remember what I said about creasing the cardboard? Now we'll use that to our advantage in creating the joints for our hand. Use the closed scissor blades to make creases across the fingers (just a dent, not a cut). Each crease will cause the cardboard to bend. In this way, we can decide where the joints of the fingers will be. For my hand, I made two joints per finger, spaced 2" (5 cm) apart. You can make more if you want.

5. Cut pieces of straw shorter than the spaces between the joints. Tightly wrap them onto each finger with tape.

It's important to leave a good-sized gap between the pieces of straw. If you don't, the ends of the straws will bump into each other when you try to close the hand.

6. Cut a 12" (30 cm) piece of string. Thread it through all the ligaments (straws) on one of the fingers, then tape the end to the back side of the finger. This will be the fingertip. (If this step is hard, try using a pipe cleaner or another thin object to push the string through the straws.

7. Before making any more fingers, take a moment to test and evaluate the one you just built. Does it articulate smoothly? Does it curl all the way? If not, redesign until it's working well before moving on.

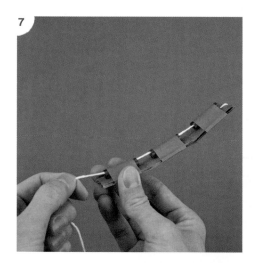

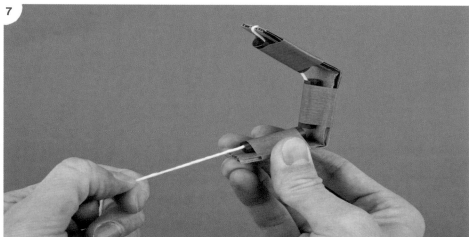

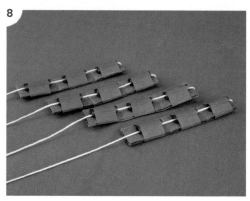

8. Repeat with all of the fingers!
Test and evaluate each one, and redesign if necessary. It's much easier to fix a finger before it's attached to the hand.

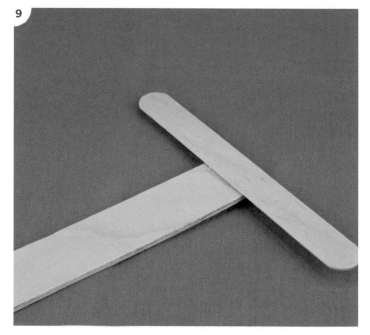

9. Center and hot glue a 6" (15 cm) craft stick crosswise onto the end of the paint stirrer, to make a T-shape. This stick will be the palm for your fingers.

10. Get ready to attach the fingers. Apply a very small dot of glue onto the end of the finger, opposite the fingertip. By using very small amounts of glue, you will have an easier time redesigning the finger arrangement later if needed.

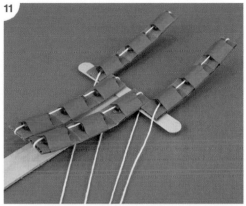

11. Choose the arrangement for your fingers and set them into place, ligament-side up. I arranged mine so that the two outer fingers face forward, and the two inner fingers face backward. This will allow them to curl in toward each other. I arranged my fingers to interlock, so they won't bump into each other, but you could also try positioning the fingers so the tips pinch together!

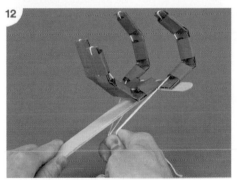

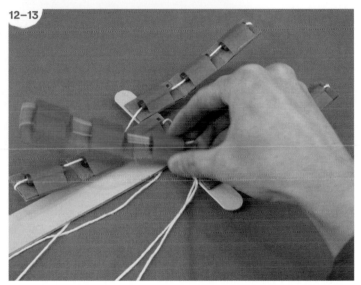

PROCESS: TEST, EVALUATE, AND REDESIGN

12. Test your mechanical hand by trying to pick up objects of different sizes and weights or by trying to complete specific tasks (catching a foam ball, holding a marker, picking up a cup, etc.)

You'll notice that the hand is better suited to some tasks more than others.

Try redesigning the finger arrangement, the number of fingers, or the fingers themselves to perform a wide range of tasks with success.

Use small dots of glue to make redesign as easy as possible. To remove a finger without damaging the cardboard, grip the spot that's glued and twist it sideways.

MINDSET: BE DETERMINED

13. Innovation and mastery require effort, so when designing, it's important to be determined to achieve the best results. Even if your mechanical hand is mostly working, persevere until you've created a finger arrangement that works really well and does the tasks that would be most important to you if you required an artificial hand.

Because there are a lot of variables in this project, troubleshooting can be complex and require multiple rounds of redesign.

That said, creating an artificial hand that can do everything a human hand can do is a big challenge—even for professional scientists and engineers. Sometimes, connecting to a real-life purpose provides the needed inspiration and motivation to be determined even when the challenge is great.

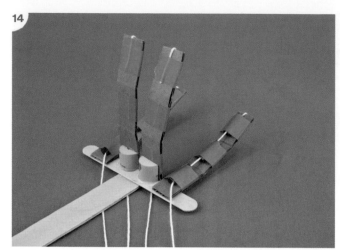

14. Try another arrangement. In this example, I glued two pieces of the cut cork onto the middle of the palm, and then glued the two middle fingers onto the flat sides of the corks.

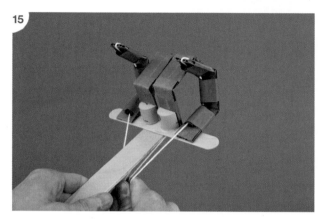

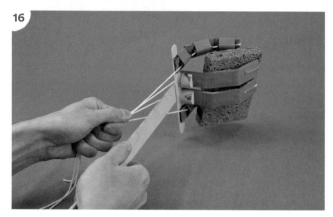

15. Now, when the hand closes, it can grasp smaller things. This works well for the fingers that I made, but you'll need to experiment to find arrangement that works best for your design.

16. Once you're satisfied with the position of your fingers, carefully remove each finger one by one to break the weak glue bond, apply a generous glob of hot glue, and reattach the fingers exactly where they were to permanently attach them to the palm. You can also permanently attach the fingers by applying glue around the perimeter of the bottom cardboard joint where it attaches to the palm.

WHERE'S THE THUMB?

Human hands have an amazing appendage: the thumb. It can move in many different directions, and is much stronger than your other fingers. In this project, we can build fingers that only open or close in one direction, so the most effective arrangement has the fingers lined up in opposition of each other. A thumb that has to be pulled in from the side won't work well with this building technique.

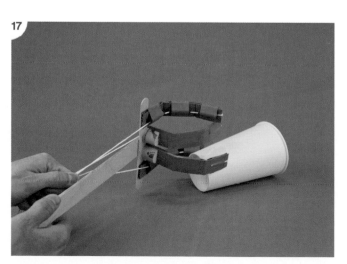

17. My flexible hand wasn't able to pick up the smooth, slippery cup. There's one more thing to work on— enhanced grip!

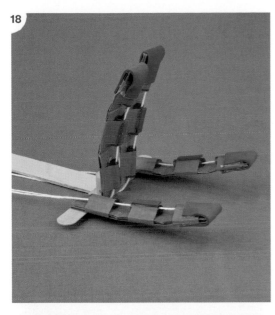

18. Cut out small pieces of foam, and glue them onto the fingers. These foam bits create more friction than the tape, which will help the hand grip smoother objects. Make sure the foam pieces are not placed too close to the joints or they will interfere with the finger movement.

As you work, ask yourself: Where do the fingers come into contact with objects? That's where you should place your foam!

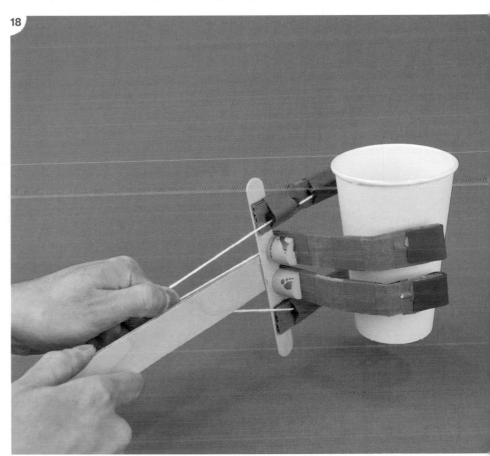

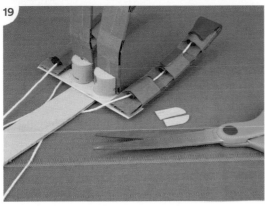

19. Once the fingers are finalized, carefully trim off any excess craft stick that's protruding from the sides of the hand.

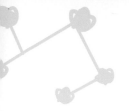

MAKE IT WEARABLE

1. Now to make your flexible hand wearable. For these steps, you'll need a buddy to help you.

Cut a 10" × 2" (25.5 × 5 cm) piece of foam. Lay the flexible hand on the table, and position the back of your own hand against the paint stirrer so the tip of your middle finger is about 1" (2.5 cm) from the "palm." Have your buddy slip the foam strip under your hand, just below your fingers.

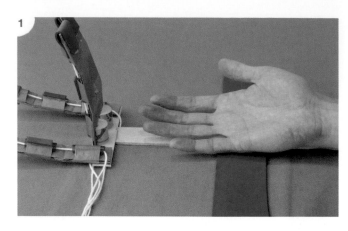

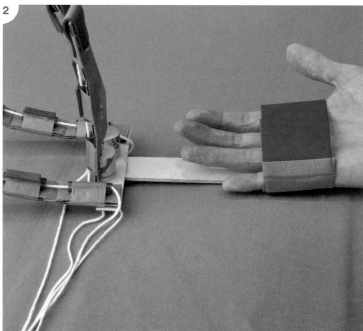

2. Take your hand away, and glue the foam piece into place. When the glue has cooled, place your hand on top again. Wrap the foam over your palm, and have your buddy tape the ends together. The strap should be snug around your palm. You may need to trim some of the foam if it's too big for your hands.

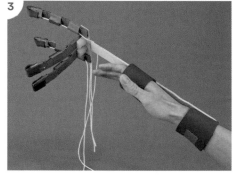

3. Undo the strap and glue another foam strip onto the back of the paint stirrer.

Put your hand back into the palm strap, and then have your buddy wrap the second strap around your forearm, and tape it.

To remove the flexible hand, just un-tape the forearm strap. Leave the palm strap taped in a loop so you can slip your fingers through it.

4. With your hand inside the palm strap, have your buddy wrap all of the strings around your middle three fingers.

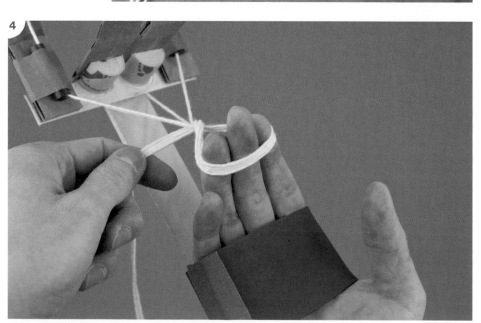